THE REVIEWS ARE IN!

M000291151

"Greg Rubano has touched 'em all in this entertaining and well researched book. A solid contribution to resurrecting Lajoie, it's a home run read for anyone who loves the game of baseball and its history."

> *-- Steve Krasner, Sportswriter who covered the Red Sox for 22 years for the Providence Journal. Mr. Krasner is now the Executive Director of Rhode Island Write on Sports.*

On *Before the Babe, the Emperor: Napoleon Lajoie* and on *Freedom between the Lines: Baseball and the Native American Boarding Schools Experience:*

"Thanks so much for sharing your books aimed at middle school youth. Fascinating and cool! I have shared them with our education team. They will be in touch."

> *-- Jeff Idelson, President of the National Baseball Hall of Fame*

On *Freedom between the Lines: Baseball and the Native American Boarding Schools Experience:*

"The book is stunning, a beautiful but horribly sad composition on the loss of a rich and storied culture. The cruelty of an America seemingly oblivious to its wrongdoing is still shocking."

> *-- Ken Burns' film production company, Florentine Films.*

In Ty Cobb's Shadow

The Story of Napoleon Lajoie,
Baseball's First Superstar

Gregory Rubano

In Ty Cobb's Shadow

The Story of Napoleon Lajoie, Baseball's First Superstar

By

Gregory Rubano

In Ty Cobb's Shadow: The Story of Napoleon Lajoie, Baseball's First Superstar
Copyright © 2016 Gregory Rubano. Produced and printed by Stillwater River Publications. All rights reserved. Written and produced in the United States of America. This book may not be reproduced or sold in any form without the expressed, written permission of the authors and publisher.

Visit our website at **www.StillwaterPress.com** for more information.

First Stillwater River Publications Edition

ISBN-10: 0-692-64986-7
ISBN-13: 978-0692-64986-2

1 2 3 4 5 6 7 8 9 10
Written by Gregory Rubano
Cover Design by Dawn M. Porter
Published by Stillwater River Publications, Glocester, RI, USA.

The views and opinions expressed in this book are solely those of the author and do not necessarily reflect the views and opinions of the publisher.

TABLE OF CONTENTS

DEDICATION

To my brother, Doug.
He never cared for baseball, but that didn't matter to me.
Some things are more important than baseball.
The best of brothers.

PREFACE

Lost and Never Found

S peaking at the 2006 National Society of American Baseball Research's conference, Chairman of the Dead Ball Era Committee, Norman Macht, admitted to ignorance and confusion. Seeing Napoleon Lajoie's name on an all-time hit list, nestled between Willie Mays and George Brett, Macht said to himself: "Who the hell was that guy anyway?"

Macht recalled grabbing his *Baseball Encyclopedia* and ".... Suddenly, it was like the very ground on which I thought I knew everything I needed to know (ha) about baseball history opened up beneath my feet. I discover that there was much more to Lajoie than his 3,242 hits... his .338 batting average... his 1,599 RBI. There was his 1901 Triple Crown, his four consecutive batting titles, and his four slugging percentage crowns. While my mind struggled to picture a second baseman capable of inflicting that kind of damage with his bat, I graveled with another question: How come I had never really heard of him before? Where was the full length biography of him, or the motion picture about his life? Who was this guy, seemingly named after an early nineteenth European emperor, who had eluded my notice for so many years?"

The fact that the Dead Ball Era was Lajoie's era and is Macht's custodial realm makes his honest admission of ignorance particularly puzzling and provoking. What gives then? How can it be that Napoleon Lajoie is only marginally known even among those determined not to let Oblivion call the game due to darkness? How can it be that those who know how to correctly spell the name of the player who recorded an unassisted triple play in Game 5 of the World Series of 1909 (Wambsganss) are unaware of the grandeur of Napoleon Lajoie?

Over seventy years earlier, in 1939, the members of the Baseball Centennial Commission were also scratching their heads in reference to Napoleon Lajoie. Their overwhelming question was not who the hell was he, but where the hell was he? Somehow, the Commission had lost contact with the player who had received more Hall of Fame votes than Cy Young and Tris Speaker. A few months before the initial Cooperstown induction ceremonies would enshrine baseball as the national pastime, the inductee who had garnered the sixth most votes from among the august celebrants had fallen off the radar. In desperation, advertisements asking for his whereabouts were inserted in the personal columns of New York papers. Fortunately, Cleveland journalists came to the rescue and Lajoie was located. He had been living on his farm in Mentor, Ohio with his wife and scores of chickens and a few horses. He had lived there for ten years to date. In this case, Lajoie's anonymity was not puzzling for chickens and horses are notoriously tight lipped and camera shy.

There are no streets named for Napoleon Lajoie in his hometown, the small industrial city of Woonsocket, Rhode Island. Former Co-director of the Rhode Island Historical Society's Museum of Work and Culture, Ray Bacon still laments that the plan to have statutes of Lajoie, HOF catcher Gabby Harnett (Woonsocket born), and star Brooklyn Dodger reliever Clem Labine (another star from Woonsocket) all positioned in front of the museum never materialized. Bacon did make sure that a small exhibit inside the museum acknowledges Lajoie. It includes a carved horseshoe made by Lajoie's nephew to commemorate a horseshoe festooned with over one thousand silver dollars given to his uncle from grateful fans on *Lajoie Day* in Cleveland in 1912.

During a swirling snowstorm a few years back, I drove with my good friend Carl Buckley to visit Armand LaMontagne, the wonderfully talented Rhode Island sculptor whose statue of Ted Williams graces the entrance of the Hall of Fame. Acknowledging his creation of Williams, Larry Bird, Babe Ruth, General Patton, etc., I asked him to consider adding to this pantheon a statue of the greatest native born ball player in the history of our state and of New England. I spoke of Lajoie's accomplishments on the field and of his admirable character. Much impressed by the feats of one hitherto unknown to him, Montagne commented that he "just might have one more statue in me." Smiling to myself, I recalled being told by an excited Hall of Fame official that if such a statue materialized, they'd definitely be there for the unveiling. With one sweeping undraping motion, the Emperor would have been back on his rightful pedestal.

Not to be.

Soon before Lajoie's retirement, St. Louis sportswriter Bill Murphy spoke to impending obscurity for Lajoie:

> *...an iron soul in an iron frame, a ball player apart and distinguished from the rest... a Titan so astonishing that he electrifies everyone who sees him. There you have Napoleon Lajoie- a man who contributed materially to baseball, a monolith of what was once the greatest pastime the world has ever known. He Is a relic of the days when giants ran rampant on the diamond. How long will it be until he too will fall like a withered leaf into the stream of time?*
> It wasn't long at all.

This is not to say that Lajoie was not acknowledged beyond his 1939 Cooperstown Induction Ceremony limelight. In 1951, in its *Jubilee of Baseball issue*, Sport Magazine chose him on their first team, all-time major league team. He was chosen also to be on Major League Baseball's All-Century Team, but as one of the alternate selections at second base.

Awhile back, a *Simpson's* episode featured Lajoie. It seems Mr. Burns is gathering a team of ringers to help defeat all opponents, and Lajoie is his first choice. The attempt is fitting since Lajoie was often called upon by town teams to be their ringer in the battle to trump their neighboring villages. Money was on the line for the games, and

Lajoie willingly took the two dollars offered. That's about what Mr. Burns would have offered. Anyway, a crestfallen Burns learns that Lajoie had died decades before. Just Lajoie's luck.

A case to consider is that of Ty Cobb. According to the nurse who shared Cobb's final moments, all Ty wanted was to be remembered. An autobiography that came out a few months after his death only for a short time helped sustain the illusion that Time doesn't have the last laugh. But when the citizens of Royston, Georgia built a memorial to Ty, it appeared that Ty would have his legacy wish crafted in marble permanence.

Not to be. Funds and visitors never came in sufficient number, and the memorial was converted to a new city hall. There is in the building a small stone tablet dedicated to Cobb that portrays him as right handed hitter. How many visitors knew the error? More recently, a few biographies and a feature film have kept Ty from floating too far down the stream of time. None were particularly flattering portraits, however.

As of this writing, a groundswell of Woonsocket and Rhode Island patrons supporting their native son has finally emerged. A few years back, Lajoie was inducted into the American French Genealogical Society's Hall of Fame in Woonsocket. This spring, the city will name a baseball field after Lajoie. In addition, every member of the Woonsocket Little league will take the field with *Naps* emblazoned on their hats, with *Lajoie* on the band of those hats. As embarrassed as he would have been, Nap would have ranked that as being as important to him as the fans of Cleveland's having honored him over a hundred years earlier by naming their team after him. Joining the swell, the Boston Red Sox's Triple-AAA team, the Paw Sox's, are considering ways to honor Lajoie and educate young people across the state and region. In addition, efforts are beginning to raise money to build a statue of

Lajoie in a prominent location in the city. All of this is part of an *Unearthing Our Treasure Campaign: Napoleon Lajoie*. Co-sponsored by the Museum of Work and Culture in Woonsocket, its goal is to develop community pride while educating old and young about a Horatio Alger success story that will inspire them to celebrate their own dreams, as well. Towards that end, all fifth graders in Woonsocket public schools will come to the museum to hear the story of Napoleon and receive a book aimed at middle schoolers: *Before the Babe, the Emperor: Napoleon Lajoie.*

Currently, I am debating a good title for that motion picture for which Mr. Macht pined. Any way to wipe that smug look off of Father Time's face. But for a moment. If ever.

This then isn't all about giving Lajoie a long overdue recognition or some kind of victory. It is more about giving him a moment in the imagination of those of all ages who love or someday will come to love the game.

In 1951, editors of Sport Magazine's Jubilee Issue chose Lajoie
for their all-time Major League team.
He is pictured top center with his arm around Ty Cobb.

Chapter One

"Pick-a-Vowel" Lajoie

In 2010, less than a half a mile from the locale of a speech he had given over a century ago, Napoleon Lajoie grew anxious as he neared completion of his remarks accepting the honor of being inducted into the French American Genealogical Society's Hall of Fame in Woonsocket, Rhode Island. Of course, the "Napoleon Lajoie" in question was a speaker who had decided to assume the persona of Napoleon Lajoie by presenting the exact remarks their native son had given to adoring citizens gathered at Monument Hall in 1900. The speaker's belief was that authenticity and brevity are good ways to be well-received by any audience. The formula seemed to be going well But now, as he prepared to say "conduct myself in a way that you will never be disappointed in me," he was wondering if in a few moments he would do just that, disappoint his audience. It was time to speak *about Lajoie*. Of necessity, that would mean pronouncing Lajoie's name. This was audience of French speaking folk, proud of their migratory heritage from Canada, proud that Woonsocket was called "the Quebec of Rhode Island." Should he risk their ire, lose his credibility by pronouncing his name as Lajoie did?

In a letter to the Hall of Fame after Lajoie's death, his niece Lillian Lamoreaux, with whom Lajoie spent his last five years, made clear that her Uncle Larry's last name was pronounced *La- Joy*, hardly a French option. For the record, the French pronunciation is *Lah-zhwah*.

Although he once told a reporter to "Give my name three syllables-La –Jo- Way," Lajoie was hardly committed to any of the possibilities during his playing career. He laughed that his last name had at least four pronunciations across the country: "Down East, they call me *Lahawah*. In Cleveland, they call me *Lah-zhu-way*. Out on the circuits, it's *La-joy*. Down here in Alexandria, it's *Mistah Lah-joh-ee*. My wife is the only one who knows how to pronounce it. She calls me Larry, sometimes real sharp."

Larry hardly touched on the other possibilities. Another option was *Lash-o-way*, allowing for slugger Larry's nickname *Slasha-way*. Ken Burns baseball documentary offered "Lah-zho- way." Upon his death, the local Daytona paper declared *Ladj-o-way* their most famous inhabitant. The daughter of burly Tiger Charles Schmidt, a catcher against whom Lajoie played for years, said that her dad insisted that it was pronounced, *Ladj-oh-aye*. A popular song of the time referred to him as *Lay-oo-way*, poetic license for rhyme scheme reasons one hopes. At least, better than *lay-a-way*, if only to avoid tired clichés about how he came through at the end.

No wonder Lajoie was sometimes referred to as" Pick-a-Vowel "Lajoie.

The story goes that as Fall River Indians owner Charlie Marston took out a pencil preparing to write Lajoie's name on the back of an envelope, he asked Lajoie to repeat his name. Larry offered his full legal name, including French pronunciation of his last. "I don't get it," said Marston. "Spell it." When Larry did, Marston replied, "Spells like La-joy to me. Well, what you call yourself doesn't matter. I am interested in what kind of ball you play for me." Ethnic pride only went so far. Dollars dancing in his imagination, Lajoie offered no insistence. Based upon La-joy's .429 performance with Fall River, Marston later would have gladly offered to take French lessons rather than offend *Big Frenchy*, as Lajoie was sometimes called.

However, receptive of any of the many options to say his name, Lajoie did draw the line. Walking down the street in Cleveland with a friend, he passed a group of young fans, one of whom remarked in an awed voice: "There goes Larry Lay-joy. He's the greatest batter in the world." The year was 1907, the first year that Lajoie's average would slip under .300, breaking a streak of eleven consecutive .300 seasons. Larry finished at .299. Of course, it was a year when the sacrifice rule was not in effect. "You're off, kid," Lajoie replied to the youngster, smiling. "When a man can't hit .300 anymore, you can't call him names like that."

And then there is his first name. On his contract with Fall River, it is *Napoleon* of course. However, *Larry* is the one he used in signing the grand majority of his correspondence with the public, from Hall of Fame correspondence and induction ceremony autographs to letter and photos. Reflective of that preference, a *Napoleon Lajoie* autograph brings a lot more money than a *Larry Lajoie*, a matter of scarcity. His wife and niece called him *Larry*. Lajoie revealed that he got the first name *Larry* because a Cleveland player "who didn't speak English too good had trouble with my last name. He couldn't get his mouth around it so he just called me *Larry*." *Larry* had its advantages. For one thing, it helped carry the alliteration for one of his many nicknames, *Larruping Larry*. For another, it is much more endearing that Napoleon. It is clear why his niece preferred Uncle Larry to Uncle Napoleon. Evidently, however, there was enough befuddlement that some people thought *Larry* was his given name and *Napoleon* a nickname. As usual, Napoleon found a way to add humor to things. Once when asked how he got the name, he responded, "My Irish friends insist that there is some Gaelic in me. Larry is a Celtic name."

Some of Larry La-Joy's friends circumvented all the confusion, just calling him *Poli* or *Nap* or *Pony*. But then many friends and admirers in Woonsocket called him Sandy. Enough is enough. That story can be told later. As for his nicknames as a player, he again filled the cup to the brim. Some of Lajoie's nicknames:

The King of Baseball
The Emperor of the Diamond
D'Artagnan of the Diamond
Old Slashaway
Larruping Larry
The Slugging Cabby
The Woonsocket Wonder

Big Frenchy
The French Devil

It is amazing that Napoleon Lajoie did not have an identity crisis. Far from it.

Early Addie Joss baseball card.

CHAPTER TWO

Nothing Gold Can Stay

I n baseball history, 11 pitchers have in the ninth inning lost perfect games. In a game known for the ways it can break hearts, Addie Joss in 1908 accomplished the feat of complete mastery with an incapacitating potion of but 74 pitches.

Just as they are today, baseball players then were superstitious. No one spoke of the perfect game as it unfurled. Players rapped on the wooden benches hoping to keep bad luck from spoiling the historic moment. The entreatments must have worked for Fate was inexorably in

Addie's favor that day. No bad calls, no errors by otherwise reliable teammates, no Texas League bloopers, no Baltimore Chops. That is not to say that Fate hadn't teased Addie earlier. In 1907 alone, he pitched three one hitters. Joss took these frustrating quests for perfection in stride. He took what the game gave him. His no-hitter, in fact, came in dramatic fashion, a 1-0 whitewashing of the White Sox, a game in which his fellow Hall of Fame opponent, saliva throwing "Big Ed" Walsh, allowed but one hit. Many rank the pitching duel as one of the greatest in baseball history.

A humble and grateful man, Joss had no inclination to allow "what might have been's" to sour his day. And the reality was that the game had been good to him, had never indicated that it would be an unfaithful lover. Two crowning laurels so often escaping those with Cooperstown enshrinement but granted to the mediocre pitcher or the flash in the pan player, had already been placed upon the head of the son of a cheesemaker.

On a summer day in Cleveland, Joss spoke leisurely to reporters of the greatness of the game that he loved. There is no evidence as to the locale of the interview, but there is also no reason not to conjure the scene. Surrounding Joss, Cleveland's League Park stands proud and empty, full of memories of infrequent triumphs and many frustrations. Joss sits on the grass, cap off, gently tossing infield dirt in his hand. Laughter and player ribbings. Very competitive men are at ease for the moment. The sounds of batted balls punctuate the muffled sound of balls captured by gloves with no laces, inch thick leather strips for webs. In the midst of his nostalgic rhapsody about the game itself, Joss looks across the field to comment on the sight of a tall muscular second baseman sending the ball to first in a fluid motion without raising himself to an erect position. He is compelled to speak. "There goes the greatest sight one could hope to see. Nothing is grander than the sight of a big man gliding over the ground with the grace of a panther and the speed of a deer." In point of fact, according to Addie, the graceful Lajoie had preserved the perfect game by "killing three line drives that would have been hits for another second baseman."

Addie's appreciation of Lajoie went far beyond his playing exploits. "There goes the greatest baseball player baseball has ever known and will know. Just imagine the good that Larry has done for baseball. Just imagine the great good that he has done for millions of people by giving them the most perfect form of entertainment."

Joss and Lajoie standing together.
Lajoie is center, front row, with Joss standing to his right.

Joss' assessment of Lajoie's preeminence was shared by many, but by the beginning of the 1911 season, the majority of scribes and fans had already fixed their eyes on Ty Cobb as the new king of baseball. Joss would not be there to protest the verdict. At the age of 31, a few years after his perfect game, fireballer Addie Joss was dead of meningeal pleurisy.

On April 11, 1911, over fifteen thousand grieving fans and many players came to Toledo for the Addie Joss funeral. Joss' Cleveland teammates had voted to attend, despite threats by League President Johnson that they would be fined and suspended for not playing the scheduled game that day against the Tigers. They and players from other teams, including the Tigers, were not to be intimidated into submission. Described as "broken hearted," they held true to their loyalty to Joss and risked Johnson's ire for causing disruption in baseball's agenda. Simmering labor hostilities and previous confrontations with Johnson and with owners explain some of their resolution. Their admiration for Addie explains the rest.

Billy Sunday, an ex-ballplayer turned evangelical preacher with a last name from some Hollywood script, delivered the funeral oration. Although hardly a Jonathan Edwards' sermon describing the imperiled soul as dangling like a spider over hell, Sunday's remarks were admonitory. Predictably, he used baseball metaphors fit for the occasion. Lamenting that "No more will the umpire walk in front of the grandstands and cry out the name of Addie Joss," Sunday acknowledged that with the bases full and the game tied with two out, a grim and determined Joss had tried hard to strike out Death. All effort was futile, however, and before ball four could be announced, "the great manager of the Universe" took the star Nap hurler out of the box and sent him to the clubhouse. "All we can hope for," Sunday concluded, "is that when the official scorers balance our averages, they will be found in our favor and make us eligible to leave the minor leagues of this world and play in God's park."

The fact was that the players had lost one of their own, and neither Addie's youth nor his skill had made a difference. Neither had his affability and decency. His peers came now to do what they did best for they understood that was all they could do. Reverend Sunday's warnings withstanding, as the twenty stars of the American League and the players of the Cleveland team took the field, some might have maintained the delusion that their youth and skill were cloaks of invincibility. The Old Boy might have a great fastball, one that he aimed at their unprotected heads, but he couldn't account for their dexterity and savvy. A few years later, he would invade their gladiatorial arena, step brazenly onto what they thought was their holy ground. Ironically, his team of choice would again be Cleveland. In 1917, Cleveland shortstop Ray Chapman was killed by a spitball, a pitch whose movement was impossible to predict, an appropriate weapon for the Wily One to dismantle the smugness of all who felt secure in their present mortality. Chapman remains the only major league player killed by a pitched ball. Ever voracious, however, Death used sports as an essential part of his strategy as recruiters trumpeted World War I as the opportunity to play in "the Greatest Game of them all." The resulting horrific loss of life easily would have filled all stadiums in both leagues.

On a warm June day about two months after the funeral, Ty Cobb came to Cleveland League Park, joining a cavalcade of American League stars, including Walter Johnson, Tris Speaker, Home Run Baker and Smoky Wood, Cy Young, and Napoleon Lajoie. Considered by some the first All-Star game ever played, seven future Hall of Famers participated. The game, however, was not a showcase intended to promote the fiscal interests of those associated with America's Game. No one received compensations; no outside pockets were lined. The Cleveland team leased out the park free of cost. All participants, including the players and League Park workers and ground crew members, volunteered their services.

Cleveland secretary E.S.Barnard, issued a statement after the game:"It seemed as if every player in the league were anxious to show how much he loved Joss by doing something to help in making the day a success. If all the volunteers who offered their services for the Joss day could have been accepted, we would have had enough players to furnish several teams. It merely went to show how universally Addie was esteemed by his fellow players." Barnard added that "To everyone who took part in Addie Joss day, whether in the spectacular role of player or the more humble province of mere spectator, must come the satisfaction of knowing that he has done his part however obscure in bringing about the day when baseball shall not be selfish nor grasping in any sense, but kind and generous and beneficent as becomes the favorite pastime of the most generous people in the world."

Each player that day knew that Addie Joss' widow, Lilian, and his two children, eight-year-old Norman and four-year-old Ruth, would need more than consoling proclamations of respect for Addie. In 1911, the average ballplayer made $7,500. No long term guaranteed contracts existed. No social security benefits would soften the blow. The Joss family would be in hard straits. In fact, the benefit game would raise over $12,000, providing the family a small measure of fiscal security.

Pragmatism and compassion aside, the players were honoring one of the very best in their fraternity, as Joss' Hall of Fame plaque confirms. Citing his league leading 27 victories and three one hitters in 1907, his four consecutive 20 or more game victory seasons and his forty-five shutouts as evident, he is described as "one of the premier pitchers of the American League's first decade." Of course, his perfect game in 1908 and his no hitter in 1910 added to his laurels. Joss' career ERA of 1.89 remains the second lowest in baseball history

As Bernard's comments made clear, Joss' playing accomplishments were only part of the story, however. A full page, 72 font poem in the Cleveland Plain Dealer a few years earlier made clear the basis of the love and respect rendered him by fans and players alike:

> *Who when his fielders make a slip*
> *Is never known to lose his grip*
> *But keeps the stiffest lip?*
> > *Our Addie*
> *And for good nature takes the bun,*
> *Is always bubbling o'er with fun-*
> *Who's is the king-pin for my mon?*
> > *Our Addie*
> *Who never condescends to brawl*
> *When umpires call a strike a ball*
> *Who is the best loved of them all?*
> > *Our Addie*

Evidently, Addie Joss was a good guy, a great guy.

Now in the Hall of Fame's archives, the above article can be found in one of the scrapbooks Lajoie kept during his playing days. It is then a testament to Lajoie's humility, as well as to Joss' decency and popularity.

A few days after his death, a poem appeared in the Chicago Tribune revealing what those across the league thought of Addie. As had the Cleveland poem, it makes clear that the basis for the respect and affection accorded him went beyond recognition of his supreme talents. His demeanor and character reflected what the game was meant to be, harkening to the gentlemanly virtues among the original clubs that had played on the Elysian Field in Hoboken decades earlier:

He pitched good ball, and what he was beside
He did not say, but showed in gentle acts;
No braggart he, nor puffed with empty pride;
A model for his kind in simple facts.
Just what he was and never tried
With vain acclaim to be what he was not.

No strength he bragged nor weakness he denied;
The best he had to give was what you got,
An honest tribute this, from one and all,
He pitched good ball

Manager of the all-star team, Washington manager Jim McAleer, made clear the esteem so many held of Addie Joss: "The memory of Addie Joss is sacred to everyone with whom he ever came in contact. The man never wore a uniform who was a greater credit to the sport than he."

No doubt then these were dark and sobering days for everyone, including Napoleon Lajoie. No player took the loss harder than Lajoie. He cried unabashedly at the funeral. "It is too much for me," he told reporters." I don't know what to say. I can't think him dead. We joined Cleveland the same year, 1902. We have been the closest of pals ever since."

One man who took the field that day was to make things even more unsettling for Lajoie. Joss' antithesis, Ty Cobb was vain, cocky, and volatile. Many accused him of being baseball's dirtiest player. He had only grudging respect from his playing peers. Many of his own teammates intensely disliked him. Nevertheless, a caring Ty Cobb had resolved to do whatever he could for the Joss family. Weeks before, quietly, he had sent $200 to Lillian and had recruited fellow Tiger teammates to attend the funeral and the game. However, once the lights were on, Cobb, as usual, found a way to draw much of the attention to himself. The day of the Addie Joss' Benefit Game, whether because he had lost his luggage in transit or had not packed his Detroit uniform believing because he was too ill to play, he appeared on the field wearing a borrowed Cleveland Naps uniform. Of course, once again, he had become a headliner.

Although not a philosophical sort, Lajoie must have wondered if anything, even death, could ever escape the shadow of Ty Cobb. As for the small matter of himself, he had just the year before, in a controversial and protracted battle that had gone down to the last day, lost the batting championship to Cobb by less than a percentage point. But Lajoie was not a man inclined to brood, and as Cobb trotted onto the field and caught the first fly ball hit to him, thoughts must have turned from the 1910 season to a decision made four years earlier. In the process, the long and sad day became more and more surreal.

The Addie Joss Benefit Game featured seven future Hall of Famers.
Ty Cobb (front row, third from right) is pictured
wearing a borrowed Cleveland Naps uniform.

CHAPTER THREE

And Then There Was Cobb

"Be good and dutiful. Conquer your anger and wild passions that would degrade dignity and belittle your manhood. Cherish all the good that springs up in you. Be under the perpetual guidance of the better angel of your nature."

William Cobb ended his letter to his fifteen year-old son with both a final directive and a warning: "Starve and drive out the demon that lurks in all human blood and is ready and anxious and restless to arise and reign."

Ty kept the letter in his wallet and later made copies. Decades later, he would describe his father as "the greatest of men" and proudly list his accomplishments, including state legislator, teacher, successful business-man, philosopher, and more.

No doubt his father's dogged resolve underpinned these successes and fueled Cobb's admiration for him. If Mr. Cobb had been a failure in life, however, that resolve would have meant nothing to his son. Early on, he had learned from his father that effort without results was not enough. A despondent seventeen- year-old Ty had written to his father telling him that he had been dropped from the Sally League minor league team. It was an eat-crow moment for the youngster. A month earlier, Mr. Cobb only begrudgingly had allowed his son to make the sojourn from home to Atlanta to test his mettle. With disgust and resignation, at three in the morning, he relented telling him, "Get it out of your system." Yet, Ty was not now summarily summoned home to await a "told-you- so" lecture. Instead, the reply was succinct. "Don't come home a failure," the father wrote back. Given an admonition and given a reprieve, Cobb turned things around quickly.

Ty Cobb's father William Herschel Cobb:
"Don't come home a failure."

However much Mr. Cobb's diverse successes impressed his son, they were not the main reason for his son's respect. The gist of Cobb's adulation, the singularly most important "achievement" of his father, was that he was "the one man who made me do his bidding." To Ty Cobb, the imposition of will upon another was the essence of defining importance.

There are a few reasons why his father's letter may have become a keepsake. For one thing, it was a rare expression of his father's affection. Mr. Cobb was a distant and demanding father. Beyond that, Ty no doubt felt that his father's words were tablet commandments that would serve him well. Perhaps they also showed that his father understood him, knew about the demons that were already battling for his goodness and dignity. They also brought affirmation that destructive instincts could be overwhelmed. The fact that he later made copies of the letter reveal that he felt his father's words could provide the recipe for sanity beyond the turbulence of teenage years. They assured him that the demons were not his alone but lurked in every human heart and that within him there was a reservoir of goodness to confront them. Good to know when those demons demanded their moment, as they often did.

One last and final conjecture as to the letter's importance. Perhaps Ty kept through the years, because he felt he had indeed lived up to his father's exhortations. Such a possibility requires recognition of Ty's belief in social Darwinism. His "survival of the fittest" ideology filtered and fueled everything. It provided the whole by which he could determine the importance of the fragment, each contest a part of the domination and survival battle. He was to say with defiance that "the honest Cobb blood …bows to no wrong nor to any man." In the process, wild passions and angers were righteous servants marshaled to preserve that manhood and dignity referred to by his father. In this way, Ty might have been an alchemist allowing his father's words to be twisted enough to confirm his own sense of righteousness. Perhaps.

Mr. Cobb, however, would hardly have seen Ty's coming deranged behaviors as confirmation that his son had done his bidding to restrain his passions and angers. The father, however, had little time to model correctives for his son. Three years after writing the letter, he would lay in a gruesome spreading pool of blood, shot to death by a woman who calmly followed her first discharge of the two barreled shot gun with another discharge that would render Mr. Cobb almost unrecognizable. That woman was his wife, Ty's mother. She thought she was shooting an intruder, or so she said.

THE DEMONS THAT LURKED

"Rarely has a more successful, more violent and more maladjusted personality passed through the annals of American sport."
Benjamin Radar on Cobb

"The most shrewd, inventive, lurid, detested, mysterious, and superb of all baseball players."
Al Stump on Cobb

In 2006, NBA Commissioner Stern suspended Piston and Pacer players for fighting in the stands with fans and with one another. Sterns made it clear that the game would not tolerate a player entering the stands to confront hecklers. Baseball Commissioner Johnson in 1912 issued a similar edict in suspending Ty Cobb for his entry into the stands to combat an abusive fan. Of course, as in all things Cobb, there was much more to this story. The fan Cobb attacked was missing one hand and three fingers on the other. The fan had aimed a steady barrage of insults at Cobb, hitting the mark so deeply that when not due at bat in the second inning Cobb remained in a carriage park area in deep center field so as to not risk further provocation. In the third inning, on his way to find Yankee President Farrell to ask him to remove the unruly fan, Cobb took the opportunity to hurl insults at the fan, including a few comments about the man's sister. As reported by manager Jennings, the fan, identified as Claude Lucker, responded by calling Cobb "a half-nigger." Asked by his teammates if he intended to take such an insult, Cobb launched himself into the stands as his teammates stood by the railing daring any NY fans to come to Lucker's rescue. When told that the fan had no hands, Cobb responded, "I don't care if he has no feet." When police finally pulled Cobb off of Lucker and back onto the field, Umpire Westervelt ordered him out of the game. Outraged and defiant, Cobb sat for five innings on the bench before he left the field. Indefinitely suspended by Johnson, Cobb was unapologetic: "When a spectator calls me 'a half-nigger,' I think it is about time to fight."

In support, the entire Georgia congressional delegation wired Cobb: "As Georgians we commend your action in resisting an uncalled insult." The Mayor of Atlanta added that "Cobb had upheld the principles that have always been taught to Southern manhood." The Police Commissioner of the city went further declaring that if Cobb "hadn't licked that man as he should, he would have lost the respect of every decent man in the country."

To the surprise of many, his Tiger teammates defended him. In a telegram protesting President Johnson's decision to suspend Cobb without a hearing, the Detroit players made clear their position: "He was fully justified, as no one could stand such abuse from anyone. We want him reinstated or there will be no game. If players cannot have protection, they must protect themselves." A perplexing interpretation of the incident. Nevertheless, unified by the collective issue created, they stood firm. And thus on May 18, 1912, the first player strike in baseball history occurred as the Tiger players left the field the minute the uniformed Cobb was ordered off the field by the umpires. They returned a few days later, only when an appreciative Cobb, fearful of the repercussions for their baseball careers, asked them to.

Knowing that they would face a $5,000 fine by the American League if the Saturday game was cancelled, Detroit had made contingency plans, scouring the Philadelphia streets for suitable replacement players. They found no suitable replacement and "suitable" soon became "any sandlotter who could stop a grapefruit from rolling uphill." The going rate for such talent was ten dollars, although the pitcher received fifteen. And so a ragtag collection of replacement players was recruited. Aloysius Travers, a theology student from nearby St Joseph, became the pitcher and Detroit coach Deacon McGuire his battery mate. No record exists of how many visits to the mound the forty-eight-year-old McGuire made, but Detroit wasn't going to spring for another fifteen dollars and so Travers went the full eight innings, giving up 26 hits along the way. His ERA was 24. Travers later became a Catholic priest. Clearly, he was on the road to becoming a sadistic marriage counselor counseling couples to go the distance no matter what the pain.

Reportedly, things got so bad that at one point ever-jovial manager Jennings instructed the outfielders to stop trying to catch the line drives and just "play them off the wall." Luckily, however, no one suffered broken bones, and no one was carted off the field. One of his fielders did lose two teeth while trying to field a grounder, however.

Sitting in the stands with his Tiger mates, Donnie Bush declared, "It's a circus. I'm glad I came."

Cobb's suspension was soon lifted, but the Lucker incident had further consequences for Cobb. He was to learn that Lucker had teammates of his own to rise to his defense and more. A few nights afterward, while in a car with his wife, Ty was attacked by a knife-wielding assailants purported to be Tammany Hall associates of Mr. Lucker, eager to even the score, and more. His back slashed, Cobb nevertheless chased one of his attackers into a back alley and pistol whipped him mercilessly. He later admitted that he left the man for death, and he might well have died. No reports were filed, and no investigation followed. Even Tammany Hall knew better that to open a can of worms.

As might be hoped, most scribes and players nationwide condemned Cobbs' reprehensible beating of Lucker and his shameless bigoted rationales, but one wonders what were the thoughts of Cleveland Naps President Somers and of Napoleon Lajoie, his player manager. Was this loose cannon behavior of Cobb the final confirmation that they had made the right move six years earlier?

Only two years into his career, the temptuous Ty Cobb had already shown both his marvelous baseball skills and his potential for self-destruction. A good number of Cobb incidents involved quarrels and fights with his own teammates. As newly arrived ball players, rookies had to have a thick skin. They could expect no civility from the opposition, nor from their own teammates. Honus Wagner often told the story of his attempt to be complimentary to a New York Giant player who was rounding second after hitting a home run. As the player passed in front of him, the friendly shortstop Wagner called to him, "Nice hit." "Go to hell," the Giant player responded. Far from offended, Wagner smiled happily. In the clubhouse later, he explained the reason for his pleasure. "I liked the remark," he said. "He was the first major leaguer to ever speak to me."

It could not be expected that veterans on the club would welcome newcomers with open arms and kind mentoring. Why would they? The "rooks" were here to take their jobs, their money and their security. No long term contracts existed. Besides gruffness and indifference peppered with occasional antagonism, rookies, however, were rarely subject to cruelty and humiliation. Practical jokes abounded. Tubs of cold water were placed under their beds that had had their slats removed. Coming back from a night on the town, frightened rookies would find phony bloodstained dead men in their hotel rooms. Scenarios were played out in which supposedly irate husbands would charge into rooms accusing the rookie with flirting with someone's girlfriend. Shoots were fired at the bewildered victim, none of whom realized that only blanks were being fired. A common game was the "snipe hunt," in which a rookie was allowed to go hunting with the veterans. Of course, to the rook this was a welcomed invite into the fraternity. The hunt was late at night. After tramping through the woods for miles, far away from landmarks, the rookie would be left with lantern and a bag while the rest of the party took off to scare the snipe towards the light and the bag. Of course, the hunting party scampered home, and the rookie wandered the forest, often not arriving until the morning or sometimes the following afternoon.

All of these and much more were harmless pranks. In most cases they were endured, understood as part of the game, hazing of sorts. They were landmines for Cobb. The problem was that since Cobb could never laugh at himself even an innocent wisecrack could be a cause for a brawl. To a man as defensive, distrusting, and unforgiving as Cobb, anything done at his expense could be deemed a declaration of war.

No doubt Cobb was not liked by his teammates. Since he antagonized so many, few talked to him. Davey Jones, perhaps his best friend on the team, attributed that dislike not only to resentment over the fact that he was "so doggone good," but also that he had a nasty disposition. He was "meaner than the devil," said Jones. If beyond their dislike of him, his teammates needed additional motivation to push his buttons, they could be driven by the entertaining emotional frenzy that followed their provocations. A free, if somewhat dangerous, freak show awaited.

According to Cobb, the players went beyond pranks. He reported that they sawed his bats in half, sneak-punched him, nailed his spikes to the floor, and much more. These acts were malicious and humiliating. It may be they created a morality play mentality that fueled and justified his tenacious responses. Cobb later contended that his teammates "turned me from a mild Christian boy to a hellcat," but if anyone ever had an attitude of defiance and paranoia, it was Cobb. He once told an interviewer to tell his readers that "I had to fight my whole life to survive. The world was stacked up against me. They tried every lousy trick in the book to whip me. But I beat the bastards and left them in the ditch. Make sure you tell them that." Cobb did not believe in suffering in silence.

After numerous confrontations with him, however, teammates learned that peaceful co-existence with this hellcat was best. They could dislike him, but it could prove foolhardy and dangerous to risk his wrath. Opposing players learned a similar lesson, even as they introduced him to another time-honored baseball tradition. Whether from the bench or on the field, jockeying was done in the hope of unnerving the victim and affecting his performance on the field or at bat. Make the player lose his concentration, and he was yours. It took many forms, most of it akin to today's term trash talking. It need not always have been malicious, nor directly confrontational or intimidating. Supposedly, such was the case of Harry Covelski. Nicknamed "the Giant Killer," Covelski was just that until the Giants discovered that as minor leaguer he had always carried bologna in his back pocket and chewed on it throughout the game. The Giants discovered this past

"They tried every lousy trick in the book to whip me,
but I beat the bastards and left them in the ditch."

secret and under McGraw's orders constantly asked him, "Hey, will you give us a chew of that bologna?" For some reason, Covelski became so unwrapped that the Giants owned him from then on. More common were comments aimed at the competency, family heritage or manhood of the recipient. Such jockeying didn't always work. In fact, it could be counterproductive. Case in point, Charles Albert Bender, the only Native American in the Hall of Fame and called "my money pitcher" by Connie Mack, flashed that impervious smile as insults to his heritage poured down upon his head. Players eventually gave it up finding that his smile did more to unnerve them than their insulting trash talk did him.

Cobb himself became quite a proponent of jockeying, as evidenced by a story told by Bill Wambsganss of Cleveland team. Wambsganss told of being showered with insults from the Tiger bench, only twenty feet away. "And darned if Ty Cobb wasn't yelling louder than the rest of them put together…. I thought it funny a star like Cobb picking on a raw rookie like me."

Players found that such provocation hardly dismantled Cobb's psyche. In fact, it usually created a heightened concentration and re-solve to win the battle of words and field performance. Eager to play such psychological warfare games, Cobb often issued the dare and the insult. Such was the case when he stood on first base and yelled to catcher Lou Criger, "I'm going down to second on the next pitch, you big baboon." Arriving at second, he again hit the air waves. "And now, I'll be on my way to third.". Standing on third, Cobb dusted off his uniform and issued the final derisive shout. "Out of my way, you ice wagon. I'm coming home and I'll cut the legs from under you if you try to stop me." Sliding home on the next pitch, Cobb had rounded the bases on four pitches. One writer acknowledged that he "never had trouble with the rifle armed Criger hereafter." It was one of three times in his career that Cobb stole second, third, and home in succession. Luckily, in this case verbal harassment didn't turn violent. It did when Cobb and another catcher, Moriarty, jockeyed back and forth. A fight ensued on the field. It continued after the game at a pre-arranged hotel room site.

Time to turn the clock back to Ty Cobb's first season, 1906. On the next to last day of that season, Cobb floored Tiger pitcher Siever after angry words regarding Cobb's on field efforts that day. The two were separated, but Cobb, calling Siever part of "an anti-Cobb ring," lay awake that night with a loaded pistol. Despite the problems, Cobb finished the year with a .320 batting average, fifth highest average in the American League among regulars, and won the begrudging acknowledgement from his teammates that he was an extraordinary player.

When energetic and fatherly Hughy Jennings was hired as new manager hope rose for keeping the fiery Georgian in tow. That hope had quickly extinguished even before the next season had begun. In March, Cobb had a run in with a black groundskeeper who, perhaps drunk, waved a hand in his face and called him Carrie. Not about to take any perceived verbal abuse from anyone, most especially a black man, Cobb soon was slapping the man, chasing him towards the bleachers down third base. When the keeper's wife began yelling at him, Cobb grabbed her and began to choke her. At this point, Charles Schmidt, a burly young catcher from Arkansas whose game time entertainment included pounding nails into the bench with his bare hands, intervened in her defense. He told his incensed teammate that "Whoever does a thing like that is a coward." The fight was on. Punches were thrown and bodies rolled about in the dirt. Fortunately, especially since Schmidt was a former boxer who had gone a few rounds with heavyweight champ Jack Johnson, neither was hurt.

Detroit owner Frank Navin and manager Jennings had had enough of Cobb's unpredictable and bizarre behaviors. That night Jennings offered the deal to Cleveland: Cobb for all-star outfielder Elmer Flick. A quality player who in 1905 had lead the league in hitting, Flick had presented his own challenge. As Phillies in 1900, Lajoie and he had engaged in a fight which resulted in a broken hand for Lajoie.

According to Navin, it was Cleveland that refused to pull the trigger on the deal. At the very least, the Cleveland decision was made in consultation with Lajoie. Despite his less than harmonious relationship with Flick, Lajoie most likely feared that Cobb's instability could not be controlled. If the ebullient Detroit manager Jennings had been unable to bring Cobb into the fold, what guarantee was there that a more austere Lajoie would have more success? President Somers rather diplomatically explained the reason for their reluctance. "We'll keep Flick," Somers allegedly explained. "Maybe he isn't quite as good a batter as Cobb, but he's much nicer to have on the team." And so a man who once had punched your manager stayed on board. If Lajoie had a crystal ball, had known the ballplayer Cobb would turn out to be, had known that manager Lajoie would never lead the Naps to a pennant, the disturbed Tiger might have been a teammate.

As Cobb's career skyrocketed, Elmer Flick's fizzled.

Any projections that Cobb's antagonistic behavior was never to change though proved to be on target. Ten years later, in 1917, during an exhibition game, he and New York Giant Buck Herzog went fist to fist when Cobb responded to a dare from Herzog to steal second, which he did spiking Herzog in the process. Police and umpires had all they could do to prevent the fight from escalating as each time they were separated they went at it again. The issue was settled that night when Herzog went to Cobb's room in a prearranged confrontation, with each player having a second on hand. They stripped to the waist and finished what they had started. Cobb beat Herzog relentlessly until the fight was finally broken up by the seconds. Ever the most intelligent of combatants, Ty recognized that as an ex-fighter, Herzog held an advantage. He took that advantage away by arriving early to the room and sprinkling water over the floor. Wearing sneakers, Herzog had little traction. Cobb wore leather shoes that proved skid proof.

In this and the Lucker affairs, Cobb had been a savage. Yet, at other times he did seem to be a victim of seeded misrepresentation. In 1909, Cobb spiked Frank Baker, third baseman for the Philadelphia Athletics. Attempting a barehanded tag, Baker received a cut on his forearm, hardly a wound administered by a demon. Incensed, Connie Mack responded by calling Cobb "the dirtiest player in baseball history." An outraged fan base threatened Cobb with death and dismemberment. Fueling the fire, the Sporting News contended that "the list of Cobb's victims is too long to attribute to accident or the awkwardness of the victim." Fans and writers across the country called for Cobb's banishment from the league, even as American League President Johnson declared that Cobb was well within his baserunner rights and saw no intentionality in the incident. A *Detroit Free Press* paper defended Cobb saying that he "was being criticized left and right and being pictured as a murderer of his fellows mostly by men who have not seen the plays on which he is being judged." That night Cobb was confronted by a mob of angry fans that entered his hotel as he was about to leave. For all their bluster and outrage, the waters parted, and Ty walked calmly to his ride.

Evidently, the Philadelphia press was quite accomplished in rabble rousing. Two years later when Fred Snodgrass slide into a kneeling aforementioned Baker, he ripped the third baseman's pants from knee to hip. A few days later Snodgrass was out on a sliding attempt at third. Again Baker's pants were ripped, but he suffered only a small abrasion no cuts or blood. Of course, what the incidents proved was that the Athletics had cheap uniforms. Snodgrass recalled that the press portrayed him as the dirtiest player in baseball and claimed that he had jumped at Baker waist high and had intentionally spiked him

Cobb claimed to have only spiked two players intentionally.
"He's being pictured as a murderer of his fellows mostly by men who have not seen the plays on which he is being judged," says a defender.

in the process. "They built it up until Baker's bone showed from the knee to the hip," Snodgrass said. "A news report went out that some fanatic had shot Snodgrass in the hotel, and it was reported that I had been taken to the hospital in critical condition. They didn't have radio then and the story went over the wires. My parents living in California heard that I had been killed, and it was several hours before a retraction came out."

One can only wonder what reports made their way west when Snodgrass again was the object of fan displeasure a few years later. In a game moved to Fenway to accommodate the outpouring of fan support for the 1914 Boston Braves Miracle Team, the Braves pitcher "aimed four shots straight" at Snodgrass' head. Snodgrass went to the pitcher's box and stood there calling the guy "everything I could think of." The pitcher said nothing. However, when Snodgrass returned to first base upon, the pitcher tossed up the ball and dropped it, imitating Snodgrass's World Series error two years earlier. When an enraged Snodgrass returned to the dugout that inning, he felt compelled to issue the booing fans the index finger salute. Glass bottles and trash rained down on the field. Suddenly, a man in a long tailed coat, spats, and top hat walked onto the field, accompanied by police. He contended that Snodgrass had insulted the good citizens of Boston and demanded that he be removed from the game. Honorable James M. Curley did not get his way that day. His grandstanding no doubt got him some extra votes. When the final out was finally registered, Snodgrass ran as fast as he could to the clubhouse; teammates reported that they had never seen him run that fast on the base paths.

Soon after the Cobb- Baker incident, writers again stirred the pot. One claimed that Cobb intentionally sharpened his spikes on the dugout steps for all to see as part of his premeditated enjoyment of the pain he was to deliver that day. The erroneous story was an outgrowth of some half-serious comments made by a fellow Tiger teammate. Only upon retirement, did Cobb debunk the story, and so it became part of Cobb lore. In reality, such an intimidating technique did occur prior to a game in the 1911 World Series when manager John McGraw ordered each of his players to busily sharpen the spikes on their upraised shoes as the visiting Athletics passed on their way to their dugout. Unimpressed, the A's marched to yet another championship.

In 1915, another Cobb episode. When Boston's submarining right hander Carl Mays threw at him every time he had come to bat, Cobb threw his bat at him and called him a "yellow dog." Fans threw bottles and order had to be restored. When Cobb returned to bat, Mays hit him with a pitch on the wrist. Cobb remained restrained. When the final out was recorded, a fly to Cobb in centerfield, thousands of angry fans charged him, again yelling abuses and throwing bottles. Just as he had done in that Philadelphia hotel a few years before, Cobb was not about to back down. As hundreds of screaming enraged fans milled about him he again seemed unperturbed, almost imperial, as he walked resolutely through the malicious group and into the clubhouse. Not a single step was rushed in concession. Ty Cobb was many things, but he was never a coward. And in this case, he was not a villain.

Jockeyed and goated, humiliated and disparaged, Cobb became that much more a predator than he was. Both teammates and opposing players reported that even before the game they learned to keep their distance, choosing to walk around him, not establish eye contact. Anything to keep from releasing the predator from his cage. Of course, that wasn't impossible.

Somehow, as Cobb's electrifying skills became more and more apparent, the Tigers became increasingly unwilling to pull the plug. Perhaps recognizing the truth of today's adage that there is no such thing as bad press, they learned to put up with such behavior from the hellcat. Indeed, Henry Ford and Cobb vied for most coverage in the Detroit press. Superstar bigots, each.

Cobb then remained with the Tigers, and a succession of marvelous seasons began. He would never again be held out as trade bait. In 1907, Cobb hit .370 winning the first of six consecutive batting titles, at the time, the youngest player to win a title. In 1911, he hit .420, his career highest average. He was to average .370 during the years 1907 to 1913. Lajoie was eleven years older than Cobb but, seemingly rejuvenated by resigning his managerial duties, he hit .384, .365, .368 and .335, respectively, from the years 1910 to 1913. These two on the same team? One of the most tantalizing "what-if's" to ponder. While you are pondering, remember that Shoeless Joe Jackson joined the Naps in 1910. In 1911, he hit. 408 and followed that with a .395, only to "slump"

Ty Cobb was many things, but he was never a coward.

to. 373 in 1913. Having these three on the same team short circuits the imagination. Not to be.

Less than a year removed from the tumultuous 1910 battle with Cobb, on the saddest day in his career, looking upon Cobb dressed in a uniform of the team named after Nap himself, Lajoie must have wondered many things.

If the trade for Cobb had transpired, Shoeless Joe Jackson (left), Ty Cobb (center) and Nap Lajoie (right) would have played on the same team at one point.

CHAPTER FOUR

A Call to All

The East Side Terrors were playing the Slashers.
Piling up hits and assists and errors,
Far from their stuffy tenement homes,
That cluster thicker than honeycombs.
They ran the bases 'neath shady trees,
And were cooled by the Hudson's gentle breeze.
Mrs. Hamilton Marshall-Gray
Coming from church, chanced to drive that way.

• • •

She saw the frolicking urchins there,
Their shrill cries splitting the Sabbath air.
"Mercy," she muttered, "this must stop!"
And promptly proceeded to call a cop,
And the cop swooped down on the luckless boys,
Stopping their frivolous Sunday joys.
The Terrors and the Slashers, side by side,
Started their stifling subway ride,
Down through the city, ever down
To the warping ways of tenement Town.
Reaching their homes, the troublesome tots
Crept away to their shabby cots.
They thought of the far West Side trees
And the cool green grass, and the gentle breeze,
And how they had played their baseball game,
Till the beautiful Christian lady came

Published in 1908, the satiric poem is a clear attack upon the Sabbatarians, those who objected to baseball being played on Sunday. By 1912, except in New York and St. Louis, the battle against Sunday professional baseball was already lost. In most cities, movements such as the Industrial Workers of the World had come to bat for the street urchins. For that matter, many clergy also had come to terms with things as revealed in the broadminded response of a Rev. Gregory after seeing a game of ball in Sheepshead Bay being played but a few hundred yards away from an open air sermon. The Reverend's words were published in Napoleon Lajoie's baseball guide. No doubt the city kid knew the truth of the social gospel:

Now, the man of God had an audience of 33, while more than 3,000 attended the game of ball. What does this mean? It means that people around Sheepshead Bay prefer baseball to the gospel. How can we explain this preference for baseball over the gospel? Is it because the people around Sheepshead are wicked? I think not. The explanation is simply this- the Sheepshead Bay region folk enjoy the game of baseball and as Sunday is the only day on which they can see the game, they take it in preference to attending religious services.

Gregory reassured his readers that those who went to the game were not depraved creatures, at least no more than any who attended the sermon. They simply needed to get away from the "discipline of business" and the grit of the mills. He concluded that just as he lamented "the spiritual stupidity which dims our vision of the Divine," he lamented that other stupidity which did not recognize that the Divine is right about us in the wholesomeness of sports and the green fields and fresh breezes of the outdoors.

In a time in which workers worked 6 days a week, preserving the precious relaxation of Sunday was recognized as a priority. Reformers, including some in the church community, were less worried about Sabbath violations as they were about the moral and physical health of these city denizens. This "social gospel" insisted that industrial man had a right to recreational leisure. Touted by many as a game that promoted physical health, as well as mental and moral character development, baseball fit the bill nicely and conveniently. As early as the 1880's, Theodore Roosevelt had declared it a "most admirable and characteristic American game." By the turn of the century, magazines, sports journals, newspapers, league publications, etc., trumpeted the qualities of mind and spirit that the game fostered. Victory on the field was said to be brought about by decisiveness, quick thinking, physical conditioning, cooperation, and self-reliance. Youth companion magazines featured baseball playing role models. Protagonist heroes such as Frank Merriwell, Fred Fearnot and Jack Standfast displayed their namesake traits as they battled forces of greed, laziness and deception. Seen as a morally and physically invigorating activity, baseball was incorporated into prison rehabilitation programs promoting eventual re-introduction into society. By 1914, both San Quentin and Sing Sing had teams and the Atlanta Penitentiary team, which included the son of author Nathaniel Hawthorne, was part of an eight club league.

The love fest could be exaggerated, of course. Federick Parnly declared that baseball, not food or fuel resources, would win World War I for through it the American people have developed the necessary quick-thinking, cooperation, and qualities of mind that will defeat the Teutonic mentality.

All of this is not to say that earlier professional baseball players were applauded or that the game was highly esteemed. Just the opposite. Secretary of the Boston Braves, William "Hap" Hapgood recalls taking his players on exhibition junkets into New England towns so remote that "Rand and McNally are still looking for them." The hope was that somewhere beneath the prickly bushes, yokel baseball talent could be discovered.

Hap remembered that in one town the minister called a church meeting and prayed for rain so that the wicked professional players could not play an ungodly game intended to rook the natives out of their hard

In a mining camp, boys display their cherished possessions, a gun and a baseball bat.

earned money. Of course, the behavior of Hapgood's charges didn't help matters. In one town, they grew their hair into unruly beards and "strolled barefoot down Main Street past architecture that was as primitive as the inhabitants."

Players considering baseball as a vocation were often actively discouraged by their parents. Robert Todd Lincoln frowned upon his daughter's choice of a baseball player for a spouse calling them "a collection of buffoons." Ty Cobb's father warned him that baseball was "mere muscle work... full of no-accounts who drank and gambled and ran after lewd women." He was not so wrong. Drinking was prevalent among the players, a good number were alcoholics, and gambling was a constant side line activity. As for lewd ladies, teams were plagued by such designing women. Called "Baseball Sadies," the latter sometimes trapped or blackmailed those who enjoyed their favors. In a tragic incident, Chick Stahl of the Red Sox, distraught over fear of exposure, drank carbolic acid and died in agony at the age of thirty-four.

Lajoie was a street urchin, but he was no buffoon, no moral dissolute. He was a hardworking youth eager to use his baseball talents as a way to earn money. Hapgood could attest to Lajoie's mercenary behavior. Hapgood was called upon by a friend to provide an outside player that might make a difference for the Fisherville Foxes in their rivalry against Milbury. In those days, teams were allowed to import one such player. Since local pride and money were on the line, it was important that this outsider be a difference maker, Hapgood had heard of Lajoie's prowess and invited him up to Boston to talk. Lajoie agreed, insisting upon being compensated for the dollar-sixty trip by rail. Ever generous, Hapgood agreed, mentioning that he would in fact provide Lajoie with a five-dollar allowance as well. Lajoie arrived and twenty years later Hapgood still remembered the sight:

A big fellow, sure enough, and solemn looking duck for a youngster. He had a coachman's high hat and a long driving coat with brass buttons, everything but the whip. I'm sure he left that home with a friend. Anyway, he said he was the ball player I had written to. I told him I had some work to attend to

first and would he go down the street and take the trolley to the
field at Holy Cross. But, no sir, he wasn't going a wandering
in a strange town like that.

After seeing him hit a couple of home runs and some extra base hits to lead Fisherville to victory, Hapgood put Lajoie back on the train telling him "to turn in his cab and his brass button coat and his whip and stick to baseball and make a name for himself."

The year was 1895. The solemn looking duck was about to follow Hapgood's advice, but in the meantime it seems he wasn't about to give up a sure thing; carting lumber and driving people to funerals and wedding was pretty steady work. Former newspaperman Mickey Landry recalled a story told to him many times by his father, the story of Lajoie's arrival that same year for a game between two very bitter Massachusetts rivals, Uxbridge and Whitinsville. In this instance, Lajoie provided his own transportation, driving his horse drawn vehicle right up to the Uxbridge bench, whereupon he performed his transformation: "He tossed aside his stove pipe hat, peeled off his long coat, under which he wore a baseball shirt. He wore sneakers and carried a glove that looked as if it had been through a war."

Lajoie's funereal attire might have been seen as appropriate by the beaten Whitinsville team. Lajoie had a great day at bat and in the field, took his two dollars, jumped back on his wagon and headed back to Woonsocket. He would later refer to his hack employment as the equivalent of semi-pro ball; it couldn't compare with the ease of making real money in the big leagues. He admitted that given a choice between following corpses or playing before thousands of admiring fans was hardly a choice.

What perhaps most might have appalled Mrs. Hamilton was that baseball was a game esteemed by more than the street urchins. A poll taken in 1910 of Congress indicated that all by two played the game, those two exceptions being a blind man and a crippled man. The near unanimity might be explained by reluctance of any politician to disparage what was now commonly called "America's Game." Town and professional teams were everywhere, from mining camps to military camps to railroad teams, from an eight-team league of whalers in the Herschel Islands above the Arctic Circle,to a team composed of one armed players, the Snorkey Club, to a team of one-legged players, The Hoppers. Boston had a Fat Man's Club that played baseball to show that fat people could enjoy sports. They threatened expulsion for those trying to lose weight. Fittingly, their honorary president was three hundred and fifty pound President William Taft. Taft became stuck in the bathtub in the White House several times, prompting the installation of a new bathtub capable of holding all of the men who installed it, something the White House denied until the bathtub was torn out years later. President Taft threw out the first season Opening Day pitch to Walter Johnson and attended fourteen games while in office.

*Immense crowd in Philadelphia awaiting the next posting
on the new electronic scoreboard, 1907.*

If I'm somewhat hanky panky for a game that's strictly Yankee

When I have explained myself you will blame me not at all.

We as barefoot kids have played it and the fact should be paraded.

There is nothing like our own baseball.

I'm as dippy and as daffy as a daffodil in May

When the heroes of the diamond come on the field to play.

Then it's hats off to old Mike Donlin. To Wagner, Lajoie, and Cobb.

And we hold first place in our Yankee hearts for the stars of the National Game.

-- Stars of the National Game, 1908

Baseball shone its light through cracks in barn doors, into coal mines, onto city streets and railroad tracks, into smoky political corridors, and onto gleaming polished desks. From all walks of life and all stations, Americans answered the call. America was unabashedly in love with baseball.

According to a paper of the day, America's obsession with baseball was so extreme "that the affairs of life and state were speedily cast aside." The paper noted that on a day when a vice-presidential candidate was chosen and William Jennings Bryant gave a speech against trusts, the front page of the Pittsburgh, New York, and Chicago papers covered the three-way race among those teams. The paper also noted that news of the victories of the New York Nationals over the Pittsburgh team were sent 10,000 miles by telegraph and cable to "the Yankee tars of the fleet in Australian waters." In the meantime, scores of important games appear daily in London and Paris newspapers.

The fact was that baseball had carefully crafted its appeal to be as broad and inclusive as possible. In whatever guise, however, that appeal was based upon a call to all youth of all levels to test their mettle. There was romance to such a call. To promote that romance, baseball was to craft the game as a seductive cocktail of manliness, intelligence and scientific strategy.

Baseball's portfolio of appealing heroic types was deep. Honus Wagner played the comic rustic, the man with home spun tales of the early days. Even upon induction in Cooperstown in 1939, Wagner would remain true to his depiction. He talked of walking sixteen miles to see Connie Mack play and depicted Cooperstown as" a Sleepy Hollow kind of town, a restful place to store memories." Wagner's sparkling wit was developed in the anthracite darkness of the mines, a breeding ground for a good number of players desperate to find an alternative to that grim life. In *The Glory of Their Times*, Hall of Fame pitcher Stanley Coveleski speaks of such a life: "When I was twelve, in 1902, I was working in the mines from seven in the morning to seven at night. For those 72 hours, I got paid $3.75 a week, that's five cents an hour." Coveleski then rarely played baseball, especially in broad daylight. He joked that he would have been a natural for night baseball. Entertainment for the young Polish kid was throwing rocks at tin cans. He unerringly hit them all, even at night. Today, night games are played at the stadium named in Coveleski's honor; Coveleski Stadium is a baseball stadium in South Bend, Indiana, home to the South Bend Cubs, a minor league baseball team which plays in the Class-A Midwest League.

Sober and religious, Cy Young completed that heartland appeal of Wagner -- in this case, a farmer with a moral bearing that suggested he understood more than he said. Eddie Collins was the college smart bringing scientific knowledge to the game. Together with Christy Mathewson, Harvard Eddie Grant, and "transformers of the game," he represented a steady influx of college educated men who were there to tame the pastime's rowdiness, drive out its ruffians. Such types were "clear brained" and "clear eyed." In other words, smart and sober. Collins played with the spunk of Dustin Pedroia, and Mathewson was seen as a gentleman on and off the field. A checker playing phenom who took on teammates and fans, he was loved by all and was modest to a fault. The majority of this breed of transformers then carried no superiority or social class arrogance to a game that proclaimed its egalitarian roots. Not all. Shoeless Joe Jackson was the raw and untutored force- power given as a natural gift. Once a fan yelled out derisively to the illiterate Jackson, "How do you spell 'cat'?" Joe yelled back, "How do you spell 'shit'?" A victim of a different kind of prejudice, Native American Olympic champion Jim Thorpe was the primitive inspired by something not found in the city.

Then there were the comic heroes, the spirits who lived outside of rules, the Peter Pan boys who never grown up. Germany Schaefer comes to mind immediately. Asked to pinch hit against the White Sox, he walked to the batter's box, turned, took off his cap and spoke to the grandstand fans. "Ladies and gentleman," he announced, "you are now looking at Herman Schaefer, better known as 'Herman the Great,' acknowledged by one and all to be the greatest pinch hitter in the world. I am now going to hit the ball into the left field bleachers. Thank you." Since Schaefer's career home run to total to date was two or three, raspberry catcalls rained down upon him. Herman the Great proceeded to do what he had proclaimed- a shot into the left field bleachers. He stood at home plate until the ball cleared the bleacher fence, jumped into the air, and then ran as fast as he could to first base whereupon he announced "Schaefer leads at the Quarter pole." Off to second he ran, and announced his arrival: "Schaefer leads at the Half." After he slid into home, he announced, "Schaefer wins by a nose." He donned his cap and walked again to the grandstand. "Ladies and gentleman, thank you for your kind attention."

Players on the bench loved the show. A few years later, they were shaking their heads in disbelief. With a runner on third, Schaefer took off like a madman for second base, assuming the throw would go through and the runner could dash for home. The catcher just held the ball and Schaefer slide in uncontested. With the next pitch, Schaefer screamed "Let's try that again." He took off for first. The first baseman felt no need to cover the bag, and again the catcher held the ball. A befuddled umpire crew finally decided there was no rule against stealing first. Schaefer tried to steal second a second time on the next pitch. The catcher had been beaten into submission and threw the ball down. Both Schaefer and the runner on third were safe.

*"Ladies and gentlemen, you are now looking at Herman Schaefer,
better known as Herman the Great."*

Schaefer was a beloved clown whose antics entertained teammates and opposing players, but the character of characters was Rube
Waddell. Waddell was a drinker, but he was far from being a mean-
spirited ruffian. If he never grew up, it was because he listened first to
the spirits of play. Mentoring attempts were made to bring him closer
to fulfilling professional responsibilities. Connie Mack assigned a former constable to police Waddell after games. "The plan worked, at least
for the next two weeks of the season," according to teammate Charles
Bender. "One night Harry Davis and I were sitting in front of the Euclid

Hotel in Cleveland. It was about 11 o'clock. A cab drove up and Rube stepped out. He reached into the cab, pulled out the constable and tossed him over his shoulder. Rube then carried him into the hotel." When Davis noted that Rube was getting in early, Rube put down his inebriated guardian and proclaimed, "Getting in, hell. As soon as I put down the drunk, I'm startin' out for the evening."

Waddell could play many roles beyond the hell raiser: Waddell, the circus performer who would bear wrestle any and all comers, including alligators, Waddell, the Huck Finn who would go out fishing or hunting on game days and not always return; Waddell, the child who would chase fire engines and could be distracted by jack-in-the-box toys purposely presented to him by the opposition just for that purpose, who so loved animal crackers that his roommate who shared a bed with him had an animal cracker eating prohibition written into his contract;. Waddell, the Satchel Paige entertainer who in the ninth inning of barnstorming games would gather his infielders and outfielders about the mound, while he struck out the side, occasionally on nine pitches; Waddell, the con man who carried with him the baseball of his memorable 26 inning victory over Cy Young hoping to barter it for liquor; strangely, he had dozens of these baseballs. Waddell, the conniver who would "lose" his watch charm received as a member of the American League champion Philadelphia Athletics, afterward offering a "reward" that was paid by manager Connie Mack, that somehow found its way to a bar tender friend owed money.

There was something endearing about the big lefthander. "He'd pitch one day, and we wouldn't see him for three or four," said Wahoo Crawford, who played minor league ball with Waddell. "He'd just go fishing, or something, or be off playing ball with a bunch of twelve year olds in an empty lot somewhere. You couldn't control him

Rube Waddell: "You couldn't control him because he was just a big kid himself."

'cause he was just a big kid himself. Baseball was just a game to Rube."
Like a kid, Rube had a heart that could be easily broken. Upon seeing
his girlfriend with another man and being unable to regain her affec-
tions for the night, a distraught Waddell ran from the restaurant and
towards the harbor. Suicidal mumblings filled the air. Reaching the
harbor, he launched himself into the water. According to teammate
Charles Bender, the tide was out, and Rube landed face first in two feet
of muck. "He didn't threaten to commit suicide by drowning for some
time after that!" laughed Bender.

As might be expected, Rube Waddell did not live long. His life was cut short not so much by his own shenanigans and related health issues but by his benevolence. Visiting with a friend in a small Kentucky town threatened by the Mississippi's flooding waters, he stood waist high in freezing February waters during an around the clock shift helping pass sand bags to desperate citizens. The next day a racking cough developed. Soon a sanitarium stay and death. John McGraw, ten years later, would see to it that the unmarked grave had an inscription for the thirty-eight year-old.

Davey Jones of the Tigers assessment of baseball's broad constituencies was far less archetypal. "Baseball attracted all sorts of people in those days. We had stupid guys, smart guys, tough guys, mild guys, crazy guys, college men, slickers from the city, and hicks from the country," commented Jones. "Players were draw from every walk of life types. It was a lot of fun."

Commissioner Kenesaw Landis' Bicentennial celebration program remarks made clear baseball's pitch to the country. It was a game that developed and defined unique America character that could embrace sportsmanship while trumpeting aggression. It fans came from Mudville to Middletown. Its origins were on the back lots and its thrills traveled across the ocean. It was "everybody's party."

The iconic photo of the first Hall of Fame class (1939) shows how well baseball had earlier recruited a pantheon of players that represented the Commissioner's egalitarian depiction: Connie Mack- the sagacious manager who first worked in a shoemaking factory; Honus Wagner, the coal miner and steel worker; Cy Young, the farmer from Ohio; Tris Speaker, bronco buster from Texas; Grover Alexander, telephone lineman; Walter Johnson, telephone company post hole digger; Babe Ruth, reform school alumnus; Eddie Collins and George

Play Ball – America!

Baseball – America's National Game – is one hundred years old in 1939.

From the back lots game for boys it has grown into one of the greatest team sports in the world. It has marched side-by-side with the development of a great nation.

Throughout the world baseball today is the personification of Americanism… American sportsmanship, team-play, aggressiveness.

The game has earned that standing. Behind the bivouacs of our Civil War, on every peaceful Main Street, hard by the lethal cannon in Flanders Fields, and in the huge, sun-flooded stadia – baseball has brought everliving hours of thrills and pleasure and relaxation to countless millions.

For a hundred years it has been America's pastime – and passion. For a solid century it has brought despair to Mudville – joy to Middletown.

This year, Uncle Sam is giving a gigantic birthday party to baseball.

It's everybody's game, everybody's party.

Play ball – America!

KENESAW M. LANDIS

Sisler, graduates of Columbia and West Michigan respectively, and Nap Lajoie; cotton mill worker and hack driver in a small industrial city in the Northeast.

The dress of some of these paragons is worth noting. The only one without a tie? Babe Ruth, of course, Comfortable and cosmopolitan casual-the king wears what he wants. To his left, Connie Mack, looking like a retired college professor in his single breasted suit and polished shoes. Eddie Collins, to Babe's right, dressed in spats like the Babe, but oh those ears! Completing the front row: Cy Young, end right, looking

like he can't wait to change into his overalls, wondering if the corn harvest will be plentiful. Second row, all in ties: Honus Wagner, left, looking like he tried hard to dress himself right but unaware how to tie a tie properly; next to him, Grover Alexander, dressed to kill, looking like a distracted river boat gambler, and finally, Walter Johnson, right end, looking like a high class hit man, broad shouldered, with pocket handkerchief and pinstripes.

And standing over Babe's left shoulder, Napoleon Lajoie- stylish and handsome.

And who is missing from the photo? Hint: Ty Cobb.

Of all the heroic types in the pantheon of baseball greats, Cobb, represented one that particularly fit emerging America at the turn of the century. A jingoist journalist turned sociologist tried to link the country's essence with its love for baseball: "The fundamental reason for the popularity of the game is the fact that it is a national safety valve. A young ambitious nation needs to let off steam. Baseball serves the same purpose as a revolution in Central America or a thunderstorm on a hot day. As a toxic, an exercise, baseball is second only to death as a leveler. As long as it remains our national game, America will abide no monarchy and anarchy will be too slow."

The only player who needed a police escort after games, Ty Cobb was the poster child for this explosive catharsis, Indeed, Cobb played like the street kid dodging trolleys blind to his existence. Sliding on asphalt, pushing through crowds, raising fists to the world, he was the kid who embraced his destiny to win it all, and dared anyone to stop him.

The extent of Cobb's need to be number one was obvious from the beginning. In 1905, rooming with Nap Rucker while playing for the minor league Augusta in the Sally League, Cobb was invariably the first home to the apartment and the first guy in the tub. On one occasion, however, Rucker made it home first and after taking his bath, looked up at an enraged Cobb who confronted him with fists raised. "Have you gone crazy?" asked the astonished Rucker after the fight was over. "A –fussin and fightin' like this? Just because I happened to be in the bath first? And for the first time, too?" "You don't understand, Nap," pleaded Cobb. "I've got to be first all the time." Cobb was eighteen years old.

It is hard not to feel sorry for Cobb at such moments. It appears the demons had a firm hold, early. The price he paid to be number one was staggering. As one writer put it, "He stood first and he stood alone."

A few baseball historians have proclaimed Ty Cobb to be the industrial hero, the embodiment of those players emerging from the urban grit of an exploding industrial population at the turn of the century. However much he might have fit a reified portrait of the industrial hero, Ty Cobb was not a city boy. He was raised in Royston, Georgia. Royston had no smoke spewing mills grinding away at the youth and hope of so many. His father was a well-connected state senator, a school superintendent, and a very successful farmer.

In fact, Lajoie was the industrial denizen. Although his roots were the immigrant French population coming down from Canada to seek a better life, the streets were his playground as a youth as he struggled to advance beyond the mills and rowhouses of Woonsocket.

Napoleon Lajoie was perhaps the best Horatio Alger story that historical day in Cooperstown. His commitment to hard work and his fierce resolve had helped him to beat the suffocating odds. In 1902, he was called "the greatest player Uncle Sam owns," and he streaked across the baseball firmament as bright, if not brighter, as any. That he was frequently called "the King" made clear his status. Such preeminence did not last long. Lajoie himself explained what phenomena dimmed his light. "And then came Cobb," he acknowledged.

UNDER HIM MY GENIUS IS REBUKED

The paranoid Macbeth found no rest. Although he was the new King of Scotland, predecessor King Duncan having been brutally butchered by Macbeth himself, Macbeth felt the presence of a rival. Speaking of his kinsman Banquo, Macbeth proclaimed that "Under him my genius is rebuked." Fearful that Banquo would someday wear the crown, Macbeth began his next bloody journey.

Ty Cobb was Lajoie's Banquo. Fortunately, Lajoie had none of Macbeth's twisted psychology. As far as we know, he had no plans for Cobb to be killed, no mutilating twenty gashes awaited his competitor. It was Cobb that was more to be feared in this regard.

Ty Cobb was a multi-headed creature. For one thing, his performance on the field was beyond compare. As one player said, Cobb was "the bestest by the mostest." There was style as well as substance to that greatness. Grantland Rice proclaimed that Ty Cobb, "was a cross between a tidal wave, cyclone and earthquake-fire, wind and water. Then out of the air comes the glitter of steel, plus ten tons of dynamite hitched to a spark." In addition, his demonic drive not to be outdone, to be the last man standing, fascinated a nation competing to be preeminent among nations. But Americans saw their superiority as driven not only by resolve and self-reliance but also by disciplined application of intelligence. Strategic thought, scientific observation and applied intelligence- that was what baseball was. Many applauded the game as being a science in itself. Again, Cobb was the symbol of such application.

Players frequently identified Cobb's discipline, his mental agility, and his resolve to learn what it took to win every battle as the reasons for his superiority. Lajoie spoke of Cobb's pre-game bunting ritual. Early in his career, under the stern guidance of a coach he much respected, he had learned the trick of bunting onto a sweater strategically placed at a position between third base and the pitcher that was the most difficult to field. At the major league level, he increased the difficulty of the task, bunting into a baseball cap. He practiced various sliding techniques, sure to wear a long sleeve shirt to minimize the abrasions. To improve his base path speed, Cobb in spring training put weights in his shoes. During the off season, hunting was not merely recreation; it was a conditioning activity. Walking through the snow in Canada, wearing heavy boots, with lead weights in the instep of his shoes or walking 20 to 30 miles through the fields of Georgia, Cobb was preparing for his step upon the field of competition. By season's start, he must have felt as if he was wearing the winged shoes of Mercury.

Casey Stengel said of Ty Cobb that he was easily the greatest all-time ballplayer, that no one was even in the running. Calling Cobb "superhuman, amazing," Stengel spoke of another reason Cobb was so suc-

"A cross between a tidal wave, cyclone and earthquake."

cessful- his baseball IQ. "I knew that I couldn't run like Cobb, 'said the Old Professor, "but it wasn't his speed alone that allowed him to stretch hits." Evidently, Ty shared his secret with Stengel telling him that on any ball hit to the outfield he always rounded first at full speed. If the ball was hit to outfielder's gloved hand, he never broke stride but kept going because it meant that the outfielder in question was going to have to turn around to make the throw back in. Stengel got to the point. "Here's what made Cobb great. If the ball was hit to the out-fielder's meat hand, that's his bare hand, Ty made the turn at full speed anyway and watched the second baseman and the shortstop. If he saw either of them move towards the outfield, that meant the throw was short and he kept on going to second."

Cobb was not only a student of the game but of his opponents. He knew their temperaments, what riled each one, what mannerism in the field might be capitalized upon. Such awareness can explain his great success against the Walter Johnson, the Washington Senator who was acknowledged by many as having the most overpowering and unhittable fastball in baseball history. Johnson's weakness was that he was a gentle being, much afraid of hitting someone. Cobb capitalized upon Johnson's weakness, moving close to the plate while others stood their distance. Knowing that pitches then would come in wide, Cobb could capitalize. A contemporary of Cobb confirmed Cobb's strategy but was quick to add, "I wonder what would have happened if the situation was reversed and Johnson the batter and Cobb the pitcher. Imagine depending on Ty's mercy. That would have been like depending upon the mercy of Bob Gibson. What a match up that would have been!"

Tiger teammate Sam Crawford begrudgingly contended that it was not that Ty Cobb outhit, nor outplayed his peers on the diamond. Simply put by Crawford, "He out thought everyone." Lajoie agreed saying that" Cobb's superiority was not with his arm or bat or even his speed but with his head." Cobb remained a Br'er Fox until the end. In an Old Timer's game in New York, Cobb expressed concern for catcher Schang suggesting that he might want to move back a little since he (Cobb) no longer could hold onto the bat after a swing. Schang obliged. Cobb then lay down a bunt between the catcher and the mound.

A New York World editorial in 1907 added the motivation behind Cobb's genius. He wanted not a piece of the ball but a piece of men: "The charm of Cobb lies in his head, his eye and arm, heavens knows, are as most; but when in addition to directing them against the ball, he directs them against men, then we see more than a game, we see a drama."

An intelligent conniver, a marvelously talented player, a ruthless antagonist- but there was more. Charles Alexander quotes a sports editorial that captured the essence of Cobb's field presence: "In the decisiveness that marked his coup there was an infectious diabolical humor. Cobb charging home when he was expected to stop at third seemed to derive such unholy joy at the havoc he caused; and when the catcher had muffed the ball and the trick had succeeded, we too crowed with glee to see the mind triumphant over matter."

"He seemed to derive such unholy joy at the havoc he caused."

Other writers of the day picked up on this assessment of Cobb's daring. He was said to be "possessed by the Furies," with a determination "to hurl red hell on his way to a score." Another said that Cobb was "daring to the point of dementia." At the same time, he was "linked to a mind that moved faster than one of Edison's flickers." The consequence of these traits and temperament was drama: "Whether he's at bat, in the field, or running, the fantastic twist is an easy possibility and we sit there like children wondering what miracle he will perform next."

He may have been called "daring to the point of dementia," but Cobb professed to having sixteen different sliding techniques, all practiced even as his legs bled."

For various reasons then, Cobb's play then must have been arresting on many levels, the most essential of which was captured by George Sisler, a Hall of Famer who played against Cobb for ten years. "The greatness of Cobb was something that had to be seen," he explained. One can almost see Sisler a spectator watching that greatness on the screen of his memory as he added, "And to see him play was to remember him forever."

I know of only two players of whom I would say that to see them play was to remember them forever- Jackie Robinson and Willie Mays. Burned into my memory are images of Robinson dancing on the bases, taunting the pitcher as he stretched leads, moving like a car revving its engine threatening to be first off the line, dieseling for a sputtering moment and then gone, a human being for a moment transformed the next into a blurred force. Image-- Robinson's charge to steal home against the Yankees in the World Series, the country's showcase. There was no collision at the plate. Only Yogi Berra for a moment standing in amazement and then jumping up and down in lame protest, like a runner instinctively hopping up and down after being called out at a close play at first, knowing he was out but not believing how it had been accomplished. Like Cobb, Jackie played angry, and possessed. His base path taunting, his glaring presence a loud silent retort to every catcall, every attempted spiking, and to every uncivil civility.

And Mays? Not he of the great over the back catch and return throw in the World Series against Vic Wertz and the Indians. Instead, churning legs, pistons that didn't touch the ground and couldn't be seen. And slides that made dirt form a tornado glittering with flashing spikes, his hat flying off, landing after he reemerged from the cloud, standing triumphant on the base, promising to provoke the next riot before the next pitch was thrown.

The Treniers put his "Say Hey" essence to music:

He runs the bases like a choo-choo train
Swings around second like an aeroplane
His cap flies off when he passes third
And he heads home like an eagle bird.

Say hey, say who?
Say Willie
Say hey, say who?
Swinging at the plate
Say hey, say who?
That Giants kid is great

Like Cobb, each of these players was a disturbing presence for the generations that were enraptured by them.

And Lajoie? He played the game with grace.

CHAPTER FIVE

Amazing Grace

Look at the Robert DeNiro looking tough guy in the photo. Is "graceful" the first word that comes to mind to describe him? Remember also that Lajoie was 6′ 1″ and packed 195 pounds of muscle. He wasn't called *the Big Frenchman* for nothing.

With the exception of his gravestone inscription, which fortunately does not say he died gracefully, it is just about impossible to read anything about Lajoie without encountering the G-word. The Hall of Fame made sure it would forever be associated with him; his HOF plaque calls him "the most effective and graceful second baseman of his era." To this day, Lajoie is the only player so "graced" by such a description. During the Induction Day introductions of the players, the announcer made sure the word was repeated for those fans who were too lazy to enter the Hall and read the gleaming brass accolades. Lajoie was described as "a model of grace." The announcer's later decisive proclamation that Lajoie was baseball's greatest second baseman was a little embarrassing, considering that Eddie Collins- Lajoie's chief competitor at the time- was on the podium. Predictably, one writer proclaimed that coming to the podium, Lajoie "had the graceful stride of an athlete, though he had turned 60." He actually was 64, so that graceful stride was that much more timelessly graceful.

Addie Joss' description of Lajoie as "a big man gliding over the field with grace of a panther and the speed of a deer" was only the tip of the iceberg. The G-word onslaught was relentless. The only descriptive currency of fellow players and writers alike,. it sometimes got ludicrous. Walter Clarkson, a pitcher for the New York Highlanders, told by the manager to throw at Lajoie's head, said that Lajoie "gracefully ducked" the first two pitchers thrown at his noggin. "Gracefully ducked?" Whereas most players today would have charged the mound, some on the first pitch and just about all on the second, Lajoie bid his time. When Clarkson followed with a curve, Lajoie, "with fire smoldering in those big brown eyes," drove the pitch at Clarkson's head shouting out, "Your turn to duck." The line drive knocked off Clarkson's cap. It seems Lajoie was Fred Astaire with an attitude.

Given the purple prose excesses of the time, things could get laughable, as when a writer proclaimed that "Every time the Apollo of the Park stumbles and skids on his ear, he does it so gracefully that the ladies in the grandstand bruise their gloves." One would hope this was said sarcastically. It wasn't.

"A Fred Astaire with attitude."

"You had to hit a homer to get one past him," said a fellow player.

With gracefulness came mistaken inferences. Explaining his selection of Lajoie on his all-star team, ex-ballplayer Billy Sunday wrote that Lajoie "works as noiselessly as a Corliss engine. Makes hard plays easy." In a *Glory of Their Times* interview, Tommy Leach said that every play that Lajoie made "was so gracefully made that it made it look like the easiest thing in the world." Connie Mack echoed the sentiment saying that Lajoie "plays so naturally and so easily that it looks like a lack of effort." Of course, these baseball men were not suggesting that looking easy and being easy are the same. Writers were not always so careful to make that distinction, as in the case of the one who said that for Lajoie fielding was "as easy as eating ice cream." As "graceful" bled all over the page it was as easy as eating ice cream to conclude that Lajoie played with little effort. Accordingly, one writer chose Lajoie for his Lack of Effort Club.

Additionally, with the persistent onslaught of such descriptions came misapplied characterizations. In the guise of compliments, these attributions worked to Lajoie's disadvantage. A *Sporting News* writer told his readers that Lajoie played "without a trace of emotion." Nothing could have been further from the truth. In 1908, more than a decade into Lajoie's professional career, widely read *Base Ball Magazine* offered adjectival capsule descriptions of the stars of the game. Lajoie was said to be "cool, unemotional, reserved, and graceful." If the last adjective is correct, the first three are not. To a country that so treasured the passion and competitive call of sports, exemplified in the "impulsive and impetuous" Cobb, the "high-spirited and hot-blooded" Jackson, the "dashing, out-spoken, and spectacular" Collins, Lajoie's pedestal is little more a shoe insert. Thank God, Napoleon had his swashbuckling French heritage to counterbalance the distortion

A St Louis writer was sensitive to the character distortions, reminding his readers that Lajoie's serene and calm fielding method has led many to believe "the man is indifferent and without a soul. His style is character of his genius." It was important then not to confuse style and content.

Many years after Lajoie's retirement, countless sportswriters and fellow players still felt it necessary to mention the obligatory G-word. A writer who had never seen Lajoie play referred to the way he cocked his hat as being graceful. Hall of Fame Museum historian Lee Allen described seventy-year-old Lajoie as "moving with a ghostlike grace." A *Sporting News* editor also visiting Lajoie in his seventies described his walk as "still being graceful." It was surprising that the caption under the photo of a fit Lajoie standing with his push lawn mower didn't read "Lajoie rests after an effortless hour of graceful mowing." Throw the G-word against the wall, and any of its possible associations stuck, as when a player declared that "Old Nap was the only man who could chew scrap tobacco in such a way as to give a jaunty refinement to a vulgar habit."

Another deficit to the G-word is that it may have blunted the conjuring of imagery that makes it easy to remember the player in some heroic action. In settling an argument as to who was the most graceful player of all time, choosing from among Lajoie, Sisler, DiMaggio, and Gordon, Grantland Rice chose Lajoie, feeling that "Lajoie was more graceful in the infield than DiMaggio was in the outfield and that means something." Rice, however, made clear the dark lining of being so graced: "Lajoie is the most graceful ball player we ever saw in action. One proof of greatness though is that we can't recall any spectacular play Larry ever made. He made every type of play seem easy. There was no wasted motion." Rice explained that when covering second on a steal, for example, Lajoie only used his gloved hand. He had the knack of sweeping the ball to the base runner with one motion. Rice's description of Lajoie's tagging techniques make his graceful style more concrete, as did other observers whose collective comments allow for a recreation of his basic fielding methodology. After watching the ball into his glove, Lajoie barely squared his body and raised it to partially erect position. His eyes darting at the target before releasing the throw, he employed a snap peg, not changing body position but with his arm held close to the body, shooting the ball toward first. One scribe summarized the initial stage of this fielding process, saying that "the peerless second baseman picked the ball from the ground like a sweet sixteen accepting a box of bon-bons."

Lajoie did read his own press clippings. On a few occasions, he would lecture the press for their over- the- top language. On one occasion, picking up a paper, he read aloud a particularly enamored description of his fielding: "When occasion demands it, he moves swift as the wind but never hurries. It is the flash of the panther in the forest: quick, stealthy, and true, and before you can imagine what happened, its prey is safe and secure." He continued reading, the sarcasm now clear: "Every pose is a picture. His gracefulness was innate, his fielding living poetry."

It could have been worse. Hall of Fame Pittsburgh shortstop Honus Wagner movements to the ball were described as like those of "a land crab moving with a primitive clumsiness." Nevertheless, Lajoie needed to make things clear, to dissolve the sugar sweet layers of such portraits. "I don't move like a gliding panther in the forest, and I do hurry, and hurry to beat the band, I'm hired out to play ball for Cleveland, and I'm going to lose my meal ticket as quick as I forget to hurry." Dismissing an *Arthur Murray of the Diamond* analogy employed by a writer, Lajoie gave his description of his fielding style: "I just move along and grab it if I can."

Lajoie was so uncomfortable with all the spewing purple prose describing his play because it obscured his determined and competitive resolve to play the game as he felt it should be played. The Horatio Alger street kid knew where his bread was buttered. The boy from Woonsocket knew he might find himself back at the mill if he began believing his own press clippings. He didn't need Ty Cobb to tell him it was a dog-eat-dog world, that he needed to keep barking at intruders.

For all Lajoie's false modesty and understatement, those who had played the game at the professional level found wizardly in Lajoie's fielding. Coach of the Brooklyn team, Ivan Olson, contended that it was uncanny how quickly Lajoie got in front of the ball. What was more incredible to Olson was that no matter how hard the ball was hit, Lajoie would catch it with his bare hand and with the same motion throw it to first. Predictably, Olson went on to describe Lajoie as not only one of the game's great hitters but also "one of the most effective and graceful fielders ever." In part, these exact words found their way onto Lajoie's Hall of Fame plaque years later. John McGraw, manager of the New York Giants, provided an additional component of Lajoie's fielding style. He contended that Lajoie was the only man he had seen who could field a grounder, that "most puzzling and perverse affliction of the infielder's lot," with one hand.

Building upon McGraw's quote, a writer from *Baseball Magazine* made his case for Lajoie's uniqueness:

The best of them, Eddie Collins, John Evers, and the rest, when a grounder comes their way, make every effort to get in front of the ball, crouch to their knees, put both hands in front of the bouncing sphere, and trust should that fail them, to stop it with some part of their body. to do anything else seems impossible, the height of folly for one may judge a fly ball with accuracy but to judge a grounder would seem to imply knowledge of every excrescence of the playing field, every irregularity of surface, however slight. To judge the speed of the ball and the manner in which it may strike these hummocks, and a thousand and one other details is impossible of comprehension. And yet it is this same incredible faculty which Lajoie possesses. Where another fielder throws himself bodily before a grounder, not even daring to trust his two hands, Lajoie merely ambles towards it with his long, rangy stride, stoops with scarce a visible effort and picks up the ball as it comes skipping past. And he does this not only occasionally, but often, as though it were the veriest detail of his day's work. Such skill is simply baffling, incredible.

All of this suggests that Lajoie had incredible reflexes, great instincts and off-the-chart GPS abilities. It also makes clear why Grantland Rice couldn't remember any specific spectacular play associated with Lajoie's fielding. The ball wasn't corralled to be released only after it was secured. Instead, it was a Groucho Marx moment as the just-arrived ball was told, "Hello, you must be going." Again, the approach to the ball was more a well-timed amble rather than a desperate darting to the destination.

That Hall of Fame announcer's description of Lajoie's fielding adds more to the essence of Lajoie's competitive drive. The announcer was a fan of that passion. After the perfunctory G-word description, he launched into an excited praise that hardly complemented ubiquitous "poetry in action" portrait: "Yes, sir, overhand, underhand, on his ear, on his back, it made no difference." Dexterity, determination and urgency are finally allowed to be included in the equation. However exuberant, the comments show the tenacity of the hardnosed player that was Lajoie. Lajoie professed that he was never happier than when "covered in mud and dust." He and Dustin Pedroia of the Red Sox would have been ideal roommates, each pulling practical jokes on teammates, each willing to get his uniform dirty, each unwilling to come out of the game even as they compared spike wounds. That they both played second base would have raised the competitive stakes that much more.

A popular Christmas bumper sticker reads "Santa, define *naughty.*" Similarly, it is hard to know exactly what the word "effective" on Lajoie's Hall of Fame plaque mean. The fact is that Lajoie was a very good fielder. Four times he led the league in fielding percentage, five times in putouts, three times in assists, and five times in double plays. In the amazing 1901 season, his Triple Crown year, he also lead the league in fielding percentage, among other fielding statistical categories. One contemporary player said of Lajoie fielding, "You had to hit a home run to get the ball pass him." A writer marveled that it was frequently said that Lajoie" could stop a cannon ball if only he had a steel glove." Even among more modern players, Lajoie had a reputation of playing fearlessly as when in the 1970's Dodger Wes Parker complained to a sportswriter that the shot he hit past an overwhelmed second baseman should have been a hit, not an error. "Hell, God-damn Lajoie couldn't have stood up to it."

Writing a few years before Lajoie's death in 1959, New York Times columnist Arthur Daley mirrored what many have said about Lajoie's fielding. One gets the sense Daly had done his research, read his peers' writings. Accordingly, his description of Lajoie's fielding is predictable: And in the field, Lajoie made no difficult plays. At least none looked difficult. He could glide on the far side of second base and throw out a runner without the spectators even gasping at his wizardry. Every play was easy the way he did it." Daley also picked up the motifs on the bronze plaque in Cooperstown, calling Lajoie "the supreme stylist, a model of efficiency at the plate and field."

All of this is covered ground, excuse the pun. Daley's contribution to the grace discussion and to Lajoie's legacy was to describe Lajoie's hitting as "rippling grace." He took the G- word and gave it what it had- muscles. Now images of DiMaggio's sinewy muscled arms seen under short cut sleeves come into play. Joe was "Joltin' Joe" as well as the Yankee Clipper, puncturing power and easeful movement combined in a regal package. Pick your imagery.

*"Rich bankers, staid businessmen, clerks and laborers
all looked with awe when he came to bat."*

Lajoie's rippling grace delivered primal scream line drives pass infielders who had already moved back fearful of their safety. One writer described those drives as solid thunder. And yet, the denouement for their launching was something unexpected. Lajoie confident nonchalance was an act of theatre that began to enthrall the fans prior to his entry into the batter's box. The drama began as he tossed aside extra bats and selected his thick handled and heavy weapon of choice. One writer himself seems hypnotized as he described Lajoie approach to the plate: "Watch his ease. Watch his apparent carelessness and watch his slouching swinging walk." Connecting these actions to his general playing field demeanor, a hometown writer admitted that Lajoie's naturalness "perhaps savors a bit of the town bully." None of this was lost on the fans as "Rich bankers, staid businessman, clerks, and laborers alike all looked with awe as he carelessly walked to bat." And so those who a few hours earlier had sat wearily at board meetings, who had been squinting at columns of numbers or who had felt their insignificance as they stood next to the relentless drone of machines, were resurrected, drawn up together in anticipation of heroic acts to come. One of their own was about to do great things. Perhaps a little too much Joseph Campbell, but at the very least, his approach to the box must have conjured the images of a supremely confident Casey coming to bat: "The Frenchman strides to the plate in an indifferent manner, as if to be saying to the pitcher 'I dare you to throw one over the plate.'"

Once in the batter's box, Lajoie revealed his resolve. There would be no Rocky Colavito-like pointing of the bat at the pitcher and then cocking it back to suggest a now loaded gun. Lajoie did have a protocol, however. And it was more dramatic than the "bring it on" of David Ortiz's clapping together of his hands after spitting in his batting gloves. Instead, Lajoie carried the bat into the box, and taking it from behind his hip, drew a line in the dirt with it. He did not simply take the bat in one hand and draw the line casually. Instead, he stooped over, spread his hands on the barrel and neck of the bat, and dug the line into the ground. The pitcher and the fans could not miss the dramatic signal that the confrontation already had begun. Larry then stood back in the box and far from the plate, his hands a few inches apart on the bat. All was ready. And yet Mr. Lajoie reintroduced that seeming nonchalance: "You never saw Larry crouched and intense as are most hitters are today," commented Grantland Rice. "He would stand at the plate with the bat in his left hand and take it up just in time to swing at the ball."

In his pitch selection, Lajoie again conjured the images of Casey at bat," Larry never paid attention to the first two strikes called on him," said Hall of Fame umpire Evans." He always figured that he needed only one spotted pitch, the first one." And so, although Lajoie did not put on the smug pose of indifference as Casey did as he ignored the first two strikes thrown, Lajoie shared his supreme confidence. There was, however, no lip-snarling, plate-pounding histrionics in preparation for the next pitch. To do this, especially with two strikes, was to invite the pitcher to go head hunting.

The fuse had been lit before Lajoie had entered the batter's box. It was time for it to explode: "If you eye is quick enough, watch the ball sail into the air for as soon as it leaves the pitcher's hand, it sails past his defenseless head." The end product was not a suspended poetic offering to the gods, but a line drive intended to damage all who interceded. Stop it at your own risk.

It is tempting to believe that by definition grace doesn't drawn attention to itself. Perhaps not. Supporting the view that Lajoie outdrew them all, including Wagner and Cobb, Baseball Writers Association founder Charles Hughes offered his opinion that it was how Lajoie played the game that explained his appeal to so many. Hughes attributed Lajoie's appeal not to personality or even performance per se, but to his "power, rhythm, and beauty of action both in the field and at bat." Hughes point then was that Lajoie's play both at bat and in the field provoked an aesthetic that reached into the essence of the game.

Cobb tapped into a nation's identification with aggressiveness, spikes ablaze onto the field of America's combative culture. Lajoie's fascination was a timeless appreciation of quiet grace exploding in power and agility. Each could be mesmerizing in their own way.

CHAPTER SIX

One of the Bad Boys

In 1915, the editors of *Baseball Magazine* voiced their nostalgic regret concerning the loss of "the rough and tumble" that was "red-blooded baseball." Lamenting the passive character of the previous year, when labor problems took the "yeasty ferment" out of the game, they rejoiced that "kicking, howling, vociferous objections and frequent ejections from the scene of battle were returning throughout the circuit."

And so, the magazine raised a toast: "Here's to the maddest, merriest sort of wolfing for the good of the 1915 season." Such aggressive demeanors would confirm that the player had returned to the game, players "who thought only of how to win the game, believing that everything our side does is right, fighting, scrapping, getting the bum's rush, but showing once more the true love and devotion to the pastime."

Napoleon Lajoie would have been one of the first to second the magazine's call for a return to the "merry wolfing". A few years before his death, Lajoie called for a return of the game to its roots. "What the game needs now," said Lajoie, "is a few young fellows with the Cobb and McGraw spirit. More blood and guts."

Lajoie was not endorsing fan anarchy or a return to ruffian behaviors. He was calling for a resurrection of the passion and pride beyond reason that drove the players of his time and figured into the strategies players used to take advantage of the possibilities, violent or otherwise. The combatants were not bloodthirsty but blood was consequence of their efforts. "With everyone trying to be the best, it naturally lead to keen battle," Lajoie remarked. "I've seen infielders with their stockings soggy with blood, playing without calling time out. They had a fierce kind of pride." President of the Cleveland team, Kilfoyle confirmed Lajoie's own allegiance to the code. "I've seen him with both legs raw from sliding and I've urged him to lay off playing. There is no player gamer than Larry."

Curt Schilling's bloody sock heroics would hardly have been front page news.

Speaking with admiration about Cobb, Lajoie said. "I've seen Cobb so enraged he screeched like a woman. He'd fight with his fingernails, clawing at your eyes and his spikes raking your legs. He was a demon."

Lajoie did not play like such a possessed demon, who did? However, as confirmed by the aforementioned Baseball Magazine adjectival description of him as "detached, cool, reserved," it was somehow thought by some fans that Lajoie lacked passion. Those who believed this characterization thought that he was removed from the rough and tumble.

The reality is that the ubiquitous graceful designation obscured a competitive nature that was second to none. He played the game with an intense passion and an occasional volatile outburst that made clear that he was a card-carrying member of the "bad boys, bad boys" union. The union had many members. That Lajoie didn't carry a chip on his shoulder nor a belligerence born of paranoia as did Cobb, didn't mean he didn't enjoy mixing it up. "Even our water boy had to know how to fight," Lajoie once claimed with an appreciative and nostalgic smile.

Lajoie also wore a smile when told that Cobb had accused him of intentionally spiking him. Clearly, it was case of the best defense being a good offense. Rolling up the legs of his uniform to show reporters a cross hatching of spike wounds on both legs, he identified the specific visiting cards Cobb had left upon arriving at a second base protected by a man who gave no ground. That Cobb would arrive snarling and leave snarling was accepted by Lajoie. In fact, he was in awe of such unrelenting passion.

Although he was not the seemingly imperturbable DiMaggio, Lajoie possessed an overriding governance that prevented him from falling victim to a defensive and paranoid sense of violation. A case in point. George Stovall, a Nap player who had a decent career both as a player and coach, was one of Napoleon's greatest admirers, so much so that journalists reported that Stovall didn't want to hear any nonsense that Lajoie wasn't the greatest player in the game. Such blind adulation was not the case one day early in Stovall's career at Cleveland. On that day, he angrily confronted Lajoie about being dropped in the batting order. When Lajoie was unable to appease him, Stovall splintered a chair over his manager's head and flying fists and waterbuckets followed. No suspension followed, however. Lajoie even refused to even fine Stovall, explaining, "Why should I? George didn't mean anything by it. He is a good ballplayer, and he was a little upset." There never was a round two to their battle. Lajoie could forget, forgive, and move on. He didn't always, but he could.

Guiding the men over whom you been given charge meant understanding protocols. According to Lajoie, many players hated their manager but were told to settle their differences with him or be kicked off the team." In other words, you didn't go over their head. Confrontations between player and manager then were not all that uncommon. As the Stovall incident revealed, sometimes fists were the way to settle differences among players and between players and managers.

Sometimes, however, a player found other ways to get their way even if the manager steadfastly refused to accommodate. Years later, reviewing the closest that the Naps came to winning a pennant, 1908, Lajoie revealed that his unnecessary stubbornness in handling a player had cost them the pennant. When newly married catcher Nigel Clarke asked for permission for a day off to visit his wife, Lajoie repeatedly denied the request and harsh words followed. The next day, prior to the game's start, Clarke deliberately let a fastball hit his exposed hand. Blood streaming from it, Clarke turned to Lajoie and held up the shattered hand in triumph. "Guess I can go home now," he proclaimed. A vital cog in the team's success, Clarke missed five weeks. The team sputtered and, done in by some bad luck at the end, finished a half game out. A writer declared that "the Naps folded like napkins."

Now it was 1908's turn to be added to the "if only" list of disappointments.

Lajoie would later declare that the Naps had made a mistake in making him manager. Willing to eventually see the errors of his ways, his flaws, and publically admit them, even when it meant opening old wounds, Lajoie could be hard on himself. Yet, he rarely tossed and turned all week.

Players behaving as pranksters, immature children and thugs was a common problem for many teams at turn of the century. Such behavior both on and off the field was one of the reasons baseball began its sanitizing reform effort to bring gentlemen and college educated men into the game. Lajoie spoke of players who had no patience in not getting their way; some threatened to slug waiters if the steak was too tough or the wait too long. Most of the time, the behaviors were silly boys doing silly things. One imitated embarrassing bodily sounds as patrons entered the hotel, another created a BB launcher out of toothpicks and launched them at pretty girls, hotel clerks, and of course, umpires. Those who were victorious in arriving first to the bath tub, greased the floor with soap or hide it for later arrivals. Veterans broke the bats and hide the clothing of rookies. One rookie told of awakening one night to see what appeared to be playing cards walking across the night floor. In reality, the cards were attached to a three-inch cockroach. Players badgered porters on trains, carried their pornography and ogled women, played poker into the night and in the day, placed flies on half-eaten plates of food so as to demand replacements from management.

Things could get serious though, especially when the players frequented the dens of gamblers, drug dealers or got caught in the web of the aforementioned baseball sadies.

TO OUTSPIT AND OUTWIT

Umpires today hold the fort, daring players to express disagreement, reading their body language for signs of disrespect, confronting them with pointed fingers and puffed chests. In baseball's early days there was hardly such reverence for the game's arbitrators. Umps faced a daily mix of verbal and physical abuse. Billy Martin type players incited mayhem.

Dated by the diamond shaped home plate which became pentagonal in 1900, a late 19th century rendering "A Hot Time on the Diamond," shows a Mr. Magoo looking umpire standing firm against the outrage of an incensed mob of players and fans. Judging by the ghoulish portraits of the fans ready to jump on the field, Julius Caesar had a better change of repelling his assassins. Malevolence towards the men in black reached into the moral deliberations of the family itself. In an 1896 Chicago Tribune publication, an anonymous young poet seeks maternal approval to belt the umpire right between the eyes: "Let me clasp his throat, dear mother, in a delightful grip with one hand and with the other bat him several in the lip." Understanding his mother's reluctance to condone such violence, the fan reassures her that "while the happy people shout, I'll not kill him, dearest mother. I will only knock him out." In recognition of such a potential, the Baltimore team in 1884 installed a barbwire fence to discourage fans' excitement.

Umpire baiting and abuse continued as the century turned. Early baseball founder Spalding felt no guilt for the players and fans were simply exercising their democratic and American right to protest against tyranny. Those protests could be extreme. Umpire William McKinley once heard a fan shout out: "They killed the wrong McKinley." Umpire Ellick felt that, spurred on by the kicking behaviors of players eager to save face, fans were eager "to wish you an un-

*"While the happy people shout, I'll not kill him dear mother.
I will only knock him out."*

pleasant time in the next world." Umpire Jim Rice made clear the reality of his vocation: "I've been mobbed, cussed, booed, kicked on the ass, punched in the face, hit with mud balls and whiskey bottles." Of course, all of this was before lawsuits and medical coverage were pipe dreams. Speaking of pipe dreams, a tobacco ad around this time suggested that its product would help curb the natural desire to kill the ump for a few friendly puffs "would make even the umpire seem human." Strong stuff, indeed.

Of course, umps had one another. One day, Umpire Silk O'Loughlin told his sad tale to his peer, Umpire Hurst: "It's a dog life. Worse than that, for sometimes people speak kindly to dogs. We are outcasts, pariahs, things to be abused, and insulted. Why from three o'clock every afternoon, until after five, we stand out there with ten thousand persons abusing, insulting...."

Interrupting his colleague's rant, Hurst replied, "Yeah. But can yez beat them hours?"

Umpires Hurst, O'Loughlin, Ellick and Rice had it easy. In the minor leagues things were even worst. One ump in a "local" game

THE WORLD'S WORK ADVERTISER—MISCELLANEOUS

A friendly pipeful makes even the umpire seem almost human.

Velvet Joe

Honest to Goodness Ole Kentucky Burley

aged for two long years by Nature's way—in wooden hogsheads. That's the true story of Velvet.

Judge Velvet with your eyes wide open. It is just the good old honest tobacco that it looks and smells.

But the mellow, *mellow, mellowness* —the coolness and the comfort of it! The taste! Well, a pipeful of Velvet proves more than a page of print. Play Ball.

Liggett & Myers Tobacco Co.

15c

Velvet

TOBACCO
LIGGETT & MYERS TOBACCO CO.

Strong stuff, indeed!

called the home team runner out at the plate, thereby giving the visiting team the victory. The crowd rushed after him and only by jumping into a delivery wagon was he able to make it safely to his hotel that afternoon. When the crowd somehow discovered his whereabouts and

• • •

gathered angrily in the hotel lobby, the ump sought refuge in a room on the top floor. Into the night, the crowd remained, threatening him with lynching. Finally, at eleven o'clock, the ump raised his window and announced that he had reversed his decision and that the run counted. The appeased crowd finally left.

A Central League ump named Pollack contended that he had withstood all the abuse fans could hand out. His hair was pulled, his shins kicked, and more. But then one day "a big fellow walked down to the front of the stand, dropped a bull dog over onto the field and yelled, 'Sic him!' "It was then I resigned," a defeated Pollack explained.

Responsive to the societal call, composers eagerly joined in the assassination of the umpire. "Take Me out to the Ball Game" (1908) composer, Jack Norworth capitalized upon the abusive traditions of the game. In his hit "Let's Get the Umpire's Goat" (1909), an absent from work fan screams out to the ump to "go somewhere and die." In defining the attributes of a good ump, John Philip Sousa's "The Umpire" acknowledged the difficulty of the occupation: "An umpire needs a cool and level head that isn't hard to hit. So when fans beat up his frame, they'll have a place to sit."

It was only when Billy Evans, an umpire destined for Hall of Fame inclusion, wavered between life and death as a result of having his skull fractured by a thrown whiskey bottle, that baseball began to get serious about policing the behaviors of players and fans. Earlier in the season, as aroused fans showered the field with bottles, fellow umpire Hurst reassured Evans, "You needn't worry about those boys in April or May," Hurst told Evans. "They got no control. When the weather warms up, watch out -- they are deadly at a hundred yards." Five months later Evans found out how deadly accurate they were.

Umpire Rice: "I've been mobbed, cussed, booed, kicked on the ass, punched in the face, hit with mudballs and whiskey bottles."

Shaken by the incident, American League President Ban Johnson made the protection of the umpire and the restoration of propriety on the field his priority.

In fact, though, not everyone felt that the situation was so bad. To make that case, an editor of *Baseball Magazine* recalled a game played a few years' prior in the American Association. Despite making numerous errors in judgment, mistakes in ball and strike calls, and "fearful verdicts on the base paths," the umpire was treated with "like a gentleman and czar." So courteous was the treatment of the ump that he got through the game without a serious kick to the shins and no player threatened to meet him at the park's gates when the game was lover. Clearly then, the players had a civilized and affable nature under those rough exteriors. That the umpire happened to be John L. Sullivan, heavyweight champion of the world? Totally irrelevant.

Of course, some umpires didn't do their vocation proud. In a game against Chicago, the Cincinnati shortstop fielded a grounder by Tinker but threw the ball over the first baseman Pietz's head. The ball landed in the bleachers. Pietz however pretended he had caught the ball, leaping into the air and landing on the bag. The ump called him out. As players restrained the hitter from charging the ump, Pietz retrieved the ball, ran to the bench and tagged Tinker out.

"Now, Tinker," said Ump Moran, "you are out, anyway." The call stood.

On occasion, however, umpires would try to smooth things over when they had had a bad day. Aware that in the previous against Washington he had blown one or two calls, the aforementioned Umpire Hurst tried to make amends of sorts. Before the start of the following Washington game, he approached manager Cantillion and asked in a solicitous and amicable voice, "Joe, who's your pitcher today?"

Not to be placated, Cantillion snarled, "Guess, damn you. That's all you did yesterday." The next shot had been fired.

Hurst was capable of playing other cards. When called by a player a "blank, blank, blanket blanked blank crook," Umpire Hurst asked of him, "Do you really think I am that sort of crook?" When the player responded that "Blank, blank you, I do," Hurst in softest voice said, "Then if I were you, I wouldn't associate with such a person. Git off the field."

Not all umpires thought it was their duty to grin and bear it. Ex-boxer Billy McClean found opportunity to display his old skills and on one occasion threw a bat at taunting fans. Bill Klem, a former steelworker and bartender, defended his turf, drawing a line in the dirt and daring the offended to cross it. When called a liar, Umpire Ferguson broke the accuser's arm with the player's own bat.

● ● ●

Umpire retaliation could take more subtle forms, as when Umpire Jack Sheridan refused to award first base to notorious umpire abuser John McGraw of the New York Giants when McGraw was hit by a pitch. "The Little General" was hit four more times during the game but inexplicably never made it to first base. Sheridan later referred to McGraw as a person "as welcome as the man with black smallpox."

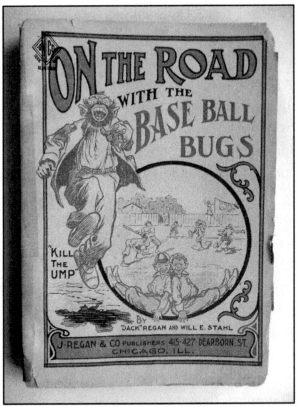

One of the most fearsome bugs encountered in a baseball garden. Fans were also called. "cranks."

Umpires were in a no-win situation. If they engaged in retaliatory action, they risked being fired or fined. They were in a no-win situation. If they "behaved," they were branded cowards by players and fans. And if they talked to players and local citizens after the game, they could be suspected of collusion in fixing the game. During the season then, the umpires traveled incognito whenever possible. And, if possible, they kept their hotels secret except to the presidents of the league. These circumspections kept them safe from abusive post game fan behavior and from unseemly contact with unsavory figures, rumored to be bettors. It was then a solitary dog's life.

Part of Lajoie's bad boy pedigree was his natural antipathy towards the arbitrators of the game. When asked why he had slugged a cabby driving him home after the game, a meek Lajoie responded, "We aren't allowed to talk to the umpires anymore. I've got to explode to someone." Although umpires generally considered him to be respectful or at least not unnecessarily confrontational, Lajoie was human and that meant to antagonize the umpire. Hall of Fame umpire Bill Klem remembered being a victim of Lajoie's anger. Responding to a third strike call, Lajoie disgustedly took out his cud of chewing tobacco out of his mouth and threw it into the umpire's face. Ironically, Roberto Alomar another Hall of Fame second baseman for Cleveland, years later spat in the face of an umpire over a disputed third strike call. A disgraced Alomar was suspended for five games. Lajoie received no such punishment. Part of the game.

Later, when President Johnson's edicts to protect the umpire were in place and suspensions and fines were enforced, player's behavior changed, including Lajoie's. A man known very much as one who valued the dollar, Lajoie dutifully complied with Johnson's policies, but purging himself of a natural instinct was not easy. One day, Lajoie confronted Umpire Dwyer, whom Lajoie tauntingly called "Blinky." It seems that Blinky, believing that a fouled ball was a passed ball, let one runner score and another advance to third in what had

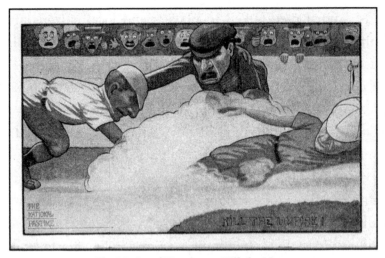

The National Pastime – Kill the Ump.
The second baseman looks awfully like Nap Lajoie with a huge nose.

been a 1-0 lead over the White Sox. Lajoie remembered that he wanted to hit the ump but instead took out his chew of tobacco, hit Blinky right in the eye, and walked off the field. Unfortunately, President Johnson was in the stands that day, and Lajoie was suspended for five days. Lajoie held no bitterness, afterward admitting that he didn't blame Johnson. He was surprised to learn later, however, that the offending tobacco chew was kept as evidence in the President's safe for over six months.

Lajoie knew of other ways to triumph over the tyranny. If you can't intimidate them, outwit them. As it does today, that might involve some trash talk. In this instance, Umpire Connolly had needed to be moved from his resolve not to remove from play the mushy thing that he held in his hand. Charging from the bench, Lajoie began with his appeal with the facts. "That's the same ball we used yesterday. It's as brown as clay and mushy as old squash."

One of the reasons that the ball was so dead during the Dead Ball Era was that it was rarely replaced. A guardian of such frugality,

Umpire Connolly responded accordingly: "What'ya think, the league's made of money?" he yelled back at Lajoie. "This here ball is staying in play. Get back to the bench and keep quiet."

Lajoie retorted, "Why you Irish immigrant, I remember when you couldn't say the word "Ball." We had to guess what you meant."

Connolly was quick to return the ethnic slur. "You Big Frog, I remember when you carried everything you owned in a $1 paper suitcase."

His trash talking over, Lajoie resorted to action. He kicked Connolly in the shins, grabbed the ball and flung it over the grandstand onto Michigan Avenue.

"You're out of the game," a furious Connolly yelled.

Nap delivered his victorious proclamation. "So's the ball."

Nap's victory was only pyrrhic, however, for the game immediately was forfeited to Detroit, 6-5.

Connolly and Lajoie had not always been so contentious. In his first game at umpiring, after calling a pitch a strike that was two feet wide of the plate, Connolly apologized to Lajoie. "I was a little off there, old boy," he rather sheepishly remarked to the surprised batter. Perhaps anticipating that the pitcher might assume that such a wide strike zone would now be the norm, Lajoie rather cordially replied, That's all right, my boy. I will go after the next one like that." Sure enough another wide sweeping outside curve follow and sure enough Lajoie hit it out of the park. Ty Cobb would have been proud of Lajoie's batting IQ that day. "Connolly never apologized to me again," admitted Lajoie.

Lajoie would later also admit that he actually got along pretty well with Connolly, although he would kick him in the shins every once in a while "just like everyone else did." Expectations were expectations.

Connolly seemed able to discount such kicking as an occupational hazard. On one occasion, however, he took on Ty Cobb, calling him out for stepping out of the batter's box while hitting. The two jawed back and forth for minutes. In the midst of receiving Cobb's verbal abuse, Connolly was hit by a whiskey bottle thrown by an irate fan.

It appears that Lajoie got along well enough with the umps to be able to plead innocent and be believed. Despite his confrontation with Connolly, he was known within the umpire fraternity as a player who didn't try to show up them, at least not that much. HOF umpire Evans remembered an incident in which a runner trying to stretch a hit used a deceptive slide to get past a rookie third baseman. The runner was safe by a yard according to Evans, but as soon as he made the call, a glove whizzed by his ear. Turning, Evans surveyed the infield. There, across the field at second base, stood a gloveless Lajoie. Evans walked up to Lajoie, speaking quietly. "You can follow the glove to the clubhouse."

Larry protested, making his point that even a blind man could see the runner was safe. The glove had been thrown at the rookie, a token of his manager's displeasure. Seeing that Lajoie was "honest in his remarks," Evans reversed his decision telling Lajoie to retrieve his glove and return to action. In reality, no one knew he had been thrown out. After the next batter singled in the runner from third, ending the game, Lajoie was heard in the clubhouse "throwing a lot of words" at the rookie.

Even when Lajoie collaborated with the umpire, the umpire paid the price. While playing for Fall River, Lajoie suggested to Umpire Cunningham that he should expand the strike zone and thus mercifully bring a long tedious drawn out game to an end so all could go home. Fall River was ahead 11-2 at the time. Unfortunately, Lajoie

"You big Frog. I remember you when you carried everything you owned in a dollar paper suitcase."
From an illustration in More Stories of Baseball Champions.

had failed to tell one of his pitchers, Wheeler, about the deal. Wheeler was a big guy. When soon afterward, Cunningham called Wheeler out on three consecutive questionable strikes, Wheeler slugged him and engaged in a prolonged assault during which he tore off almost all his clothing, so little of which was left on his bruised body that players had to form an escort to the clubhouse. An outraged Wheeler was not done. He charged into the clubhouse, stole Cunningham's clothing from his suitcase and burned it in a bonfire about which he danced madly. Owner of the Fall River team, Charlie Marden, sagaciously determined that some compensation might be due. He rented a carriage for Cunningham and paid for a new suit of clothes for the still stunned arbiter. Cunningham retired from baseball the next day, citing "the Lajoie incident" as the reason to move on to safer pursuits.

To his dying days, Lajoie loved to tell stories of the game and, of course, conflicts with umpires were good yarns. One he especially liked to tell concerned one of his Cleveland pitchers "Dummy" Taylor. Having had enough of the umpire's calls, Taylor walked slowly up to the plate and mouthed his displeasure, hoping that the ump could read his lips. He could and Taylor was thrown out of the game. Lajoie could not remember the ump's name but recalled his exact words afterward. "For a guy who can't hear," the impressed ump proclaimed, "he sure has picked up some fancy words." Some umps even knew sign language as a startled "Dummy" Hoyle discovered after his signing displeasure was translated by Umpire Smith. Hoyle too was thrown out of the game. It was not reported if the ump had used sign language to convey the message.

In 1910, *Baseball Magazine* told fans to rest easy for "Gone were the days were the rowdies who filled the air with profanity and who made the game a slugging match of brute strength and arrogance." Gone also were "the mobs and hoodlums that hurled epithets and missiles at the umpire and waited outside the park to confront the opposing nine." Baseball's sanitizing of the game was driven by business sense. It knew that if it wanted to promote itself as a family entertainment, field violence and disruption would send the wrong message. In a 1907 Coke ad, Lajoie proclaims the virtues of the drink, calling it "the most refreshing beverage an athlete can drink." Umpire O'Loughlin agrees, for "Nothing will relieve fatigue and quench thirst like Coca-Cola." Lajoie and the O'Loughlin may have agreed for once, but no one expected the player and ump to ever sit down at the same table and drink that Coke together.

CHAPTER SEVEN

Beware the Lajoie

In an early 1900's publication, a fevered baseball fan, identifying himself as a bleacher bug, reported a strange dream in which *the Lajoie*, a creature "with eyes aflame and jaws eager to bit flesh," reached out with its strong claws to clasp a paralyzed young pitcher. His courage driven by necessity, the youth confronted the beast and "oh frabjous day" he left it dead and with its head went "walterjohnsing back." Then and only then did peace return to the exalted fraternity of great hurlers such as Walter Johnson, Christy Mathewson and Rube Waddell, Hall of Famers all of whom had stood but sixty feet six inches from the menace.

Inhabiting the woods were other frightening creatures, including Shoeless Joe Jackson, Home Run Baker, and Eddie Collins, but it was this deadly foe that was most to be feared. *The Lajoie* was the terrifying Jabberwocky straight out of Lewis G. Carroll's *Alice in Wonderland's* fantastical world.

But where is the *tyrannosaurus* rex *cobb*ling threw the dark woods, his tail spikewacking the borogroves? Ty Cobb's absence is noteworthy, especially since when the poem appeared in 1917, Cobb was still king of the baseball woods.

The respect for the might of the Lajoie was not limited to the fan's overwrought imagination. In prefacing remarks to an interview with Lajoie, Charles Weir admitted to some anxiety at meeting" a man who breaks baseball." Weir explained, "I'm not romancing…This is the plain, unvarnished truth. And what is more, it happened not once but twice. So hard was the bat swung that the ball was actually torn apart. Can you imagine the expression on the fielder's faces?" The lack of precedence for such a rarity provoked Weir to ponder their rule implications: "Should the batter be given a home run?" Anticipating the incredulity of the readers, Weir assured them that these baseballs were not your playground variety, but "good strong balls, with the guarantee of an old established manufacturer, warranted." Weir questioned his own credulity for "who could believe that any one could break such a ball with one stroke. That is why I surveyed the man before me- the hero of such a feat- with such interest."

However earnest, Weir offered no specific details regarding the epidermal mutilations attributed to Lajoie. No photos of the ravaged balls exist. And so we are left with mythical images of Roy Hobbs in *The Natural* hitting a ball that implodes as it rockets towards right field. Shorn of its cover, reduced to a Medusa's head pool of yarn, it is retrieved by a confused outfielder who throws it to third base. There the opposing coaches demand to see the ball, "not that stuff." Of course, Hobb's incredulous manager admits maybe it was a defective ball, not knowing what else to say.

Lajoie with the Philadelphia Phils ca. 1895. Notice the square plate. The pentagonal shape was introduced around 1900.

In fact, a Society of Baseball Research article reported that in 1899 Lajoie on three occasions ripped the cover off the ball. Details as to when and where are not given, nor is the exact condition of those balls mentioned. In 1899, an Ohio newspaper, however, reported that Lajoie, then a member of the Philadelphia team, hit a ball so hard that "he actually broke it." The ball struck the center field fence so hard that "the rubber on the inside was broken" and the completely lopsided ball was thrown out of the game. Lajoie received a triple, as far as he was able to advance until the ball was retrieved. It not so clear how many bases Lajoie received when according to the same paper he had earlier in the year driven a ball so hard off the brick clubhouse in left that the cover of the ball was busted and the liberated yarn rolled out. The retrieval of that ball must have provoked a strange mix of comedy and awe.

Lajoie's power antics could be entertaining. Calling it the funniest incident he had ever seen in baseball, Yankee George Moriarty recalled the image of his centerfielder "hanging on in monkey like fashion" as he tried desperately to dislodge a Lajoie shot that stuck in the screen. He was unsuccessful, and Lajoie trotted home with a walk off homer. Lajoie himself chuckled recalling a time when he reached way across the plate to strike a ball intended to be part of an intentional pass sequence. He sent a screaming line drive out to unprepared right fielder Willy Keeler. The ball struck him in the chest and knocked him over. Lajoie remembers Keeler "calling him some names" upon the inning's conclusion. The diminutive Hall of Famer Keeler was also a victim of Lajoie's power when in a game against the New York Highlanders, Lajoie smashed a shot that stuck in the chicken wire fence that formed an entrance to the bleachers from a side street. As Lajoie circled the bases. Keeler climbed the chicken wire and frantically tried to dislodge the ball. Finally, he did so but the ball landed outside the park and one of the game's oddest home runs was recorded.

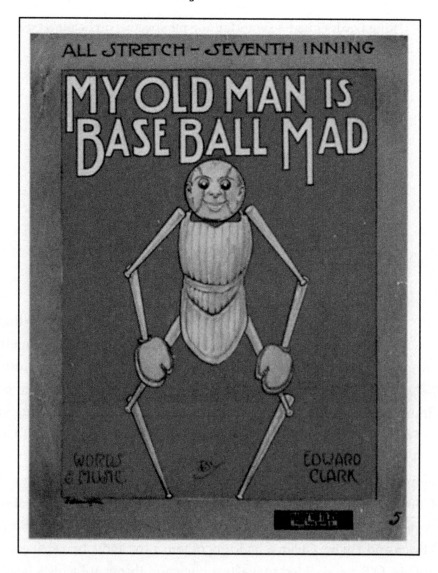

As embarrassed as Keeler was, the consequences of the slip up did not linger. Not the case for John Anderson. Also trying to free a ball hit by Lajoie into a wire outfield fence, Anderson pushed it through the fence and into home run territory. For his blunder, he was given the nickname "The Goat." The name stayed with him throughout his career.

Ring Lardner had an entertaining perspective on Lajoie's power:

"Those who are cognizant of my great age sometimes ask me what Larry Lajoie would do in "this" game. Well, he wouldn't do anything after one day. Larry wasn't a fly ball hitter. When he got ahold of one, it usually hit the fence on one bounce, traveling about five feet three inches above the ground most of the way, removing the ears of all infielders who didn't throw themselves flat on their stomach the instant they saw him swing. After the battle, there would be a meeting of earless infielder threatening a walkout if that Big French gunman was allowed in the park again, even with a toothpick in his hand."

The problem with such writing full of wit and hyperbole is that it invites easy dismissal of the basic premise that Lajoie was a uniquely powerful hitter whose forte was the vicious line drive. Unlike Ruth, *Slashaway*, as Lajoie was often called, did not hit majestic drives to be admired as they climbed into the sky and arced downward. Writing in the *Forties*, New York Times columnist Arthur Daley claimed that Lajoie's "clothes line drives would threaten infielders with decapitation before sailing over the outfielder's head." Daley supported his brand of florid language by reporting the story told by a veteran Boston sportswriter speaking of an encounter between Red Sox pitcher Buck O'Brien and Lajoie. Given a padding of four runs and a two strike advantage, O'Brien decided to waste a pitch and throw at Lajoie's head. The pitch, not the head, bounced off the center field fence and two runs scored. Next time Lajoie came to bat, O'Brien told his battery mate of a new strategy. "I'm going to throw him a pitch I've never thrown him before- a round-house curve." Lajoie sent it back screaming at shortstop Heinie Wagner, O'Brien's roommate. The ball caromed off Wagner's hip and into the outfield. Rather than go out for the possible relay throw, Wagner charged the mound. "I'm captain of this club, Buck, and if you throw the Big Frenchman anymore pitches like that you won't get in the room tonight." Lajoie wasn't done intimidating the Sox's left side in fielders. On his following trip to the plate, he rifled one at third baseman Larry Gardner. The ball split bleeding Gardner's hand "as if it had been gashed by a knife." On his last plate appearance, Lajoie was intentionally walked. Not surprisingly, O'Brien years later called Lajoie "the granddaddy of them all."

Louisville third baseman Flaherty would have settled for Gardner's injury. Prior to rushing off to umpire a game in Brooklyn, a rather paternal Tim Hurst suggested to Flaherty that he consider moving up so that he could more effectively get to bunts and choppers. Hurst awoke the next day to read the news that Flaherty had been injured in the game against Cleveland. A week later, the two met again. Standing on crutches, muttering obscenities, Flaherty revealed that he had followed the advice given him and "the murderous Frenchman had torn the bark off his shins" with a vicious line drive. A guilty Hurst and a crippled Flaherty went their separate ways.

Kid Elberfield of Washington was more fortunate in his encounter with a Lajoie missile. "I recall that I was playing rather deep at the time. The pitcher, I don't remember who he was, put one down the alley and Lajoie took a mighty poke at it. I was bent over with a hand on each knee and the sound of wood and leather had hardly reached me before I saw that ball come shooting toward me with the speed of a rifle bullet. All I had time to do was to take my hands off my knees and close them between my legs when the ball reached me, struck fairly in the center of my glove."

Elberfield paused to allow his hot corner story to take on the fantastic dimension it deserved. "And I went on. I went right up in the air and landed flat on my back on the grass about three feet from where I had been crouching. The next thing I know the Cleveland coach was standing over me demanding to know where I was hurt. I took the ball out of the glove and wrung my hand to see whether I had broken any bones in it. Luckily, my glove had borne the brunt of the attack, though my member felt numb for hours afterward." Elberfield shook his head for emphasis. "Everyone congratulated me, but if I could have gotten out of the way of that ball I would never had made the catch. That is why I say that Larry is the hardest hitter. And I shall believe that, too, until my dying day."

Even after his major league playing days were over, Lajoie could deliver the message. About ready to make his first international league appearance at Indianapolis, rookie Ran Johnson decided to use his final warm up pitches to display his fastball for the fans. Prior to taking starting the game, Johnson had been told that he was going to face some "bum." The so-called bum was Lajoie, at the time the player-manager of the team. Arriving at the plate for his first at bat, Lajoie said to the catcher, "My, my, that boy throws an awful fastball." Hearing the comment, Johnson decided to switch things around and throw what he called "the slowest pitched ball of my life." Expecting a fastball, Lajoie hitched, and then gave it a mighty swing. He hit the top of the ball, sending it rocketing to the first baseman, who had just jumped off of first base after covering the runner. The clothesline shot landed squarely in the center of his upraised glove. Recoiling, the first baseman rocked back and then fell forward to the ground. Stunned, he sat up, the ball still in his glove, his face "as white as the foul line." At the time, Lajoie was 43.

"I doubt very much if Ruth hit a more wicked ball than Lajoie," proclaimed Henry Edwards, former secretary of the American League. Edwards told the story of the young Tiger pitcher George Mullin. Mullin decided that the best way to take the sting out of Lajoie's line drives was to throw him a slow and soft one. Lajoie pulled the pitch down third sending it off the shoulder of third baseman Moriarty. Not the Solomon of pitchers, Mullin next time offered a change up to Lajoie. Handcuffed, diving to the ground to avoid being hit, Moriarty watched the ball whiz past his ear. Later to be called "two-fisted Moriarty," the Tiger hot headed hot corner guardian charged the mound. "If you give that Frenchman another slow ball," he snarled, "so help me, I'll kill you. If he doesn't kill me first."

Some pitchers decided that to confront "the Lajoie" at all was a serious mistake. On May 23, 1901, in the midst of a wondrous Triple Crown season, Lajoie was intentionally walked with the bases loaded and no one out. Ahead 11-7, player manager Clark Griffin inserted himself as the pitcher and "calmly sent four wide ones across" to force home a run. What made the act that much more outrageous was that the batters that followed were future American League home run leaders, Socks Seybold and Harry Davis. Griffith's bravado paid off when he retired these two and a third, all on infield grounders. Lajoie was the first of only five players who were intentionally walked with the bases loaded, the others being Del Bissonette (1928), Bill Nicholson (1944), Barry Bonds (1998) and Josh Hamilton (2008). That season, the Big Frenchman lead the league in a staggering number of categories, including home runs, runs batted in, doubles, on-base percentage, slugging percentage, and hits. Playing in 131 games, he went hitless in only 17 of them. No wonder Griffith referred to Lajoie as "the French Devil."

Asked what kind of pitch, he couldn't hit, Lajoie responded, "The ones I can't reach." Indeed, some pitchers tried to give the Big Frenchman a pass but somehow couldn't accomplish the task. In a game against Cleveland, New York pitcher Russell Ford shrewdly decided to walk Lajoie with two men on base. Swinging with one hand, Lajoie reached over the plate and doubled to right to score both runners. Two innings later, Lajoie took a far outside pitch and again drove it to right

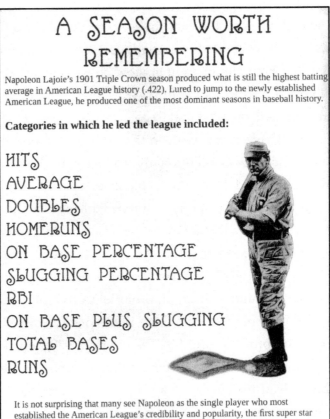

A SEASON WORTH REMEMBERING

Napoleon Lajoie's 1901 Triple Crown season produced what is still the highest batting average in American League history (.422). Lured to jump to the newly established American League, he produced one of the most dominant seasons in baseball history.

Categories in which he led the league included:

HITS
AVERAGE
DOUBLES
HOMERUNS
ON BASE PERCENTAGE
SLUGGING PERCENTAGE
RBI
ON BASE PLUS SLUGGING
TOTAL BASES
RUNS

It is not surprising that many see Napoleon as the single player who most established the American League's credibility and popularity, the first super star of the sport.

for a double, again with one hand. The French Devil got a third one handed double on another attempted intentional pass. Finally, an exasperated Ford threw four pitches behind Lajoie for his final at bat. "Now hit that one," he yelled out. Later, Ford declared to the press, "Even Lajoie can't hit a ball with his backside."

Since during the era it was permissible to step on and/or across the plate when hitting, such attempts to keep the ball in play were not that uncommon. To have great success in doing so, was. In fact, Napoleon was reported to have gotten hits by throwing his bat at the ball-and not all were singles.

Upon Lajoie's death, Daley recounted that many of Lajoie's contemporaries, "with scorn in very word," would often ask "Can you picture what a Napoleon Lajoie would have done to the jackrabbit ball they use now?" Daley provided their answer to the rhetorical question: Lajoie would have been a Babe Ruth. Fascination as to Lajoie's legacy if he had not played in the Dead Ball Era was rampant. Ty Cobb was part of that chorus: "If the Big Frenchman hit the ball they use today, he'd been the greatest hitter baseball ever knew. He always hit line drives. The greatest ever. That's what I said and that's what I believe. He ripped that ball something terrible. But he never did get a shot at the lively ball." Ty called the lively ball "dynamite wrapped in cowhide."

Almost sixty at the time, Lajoie agreed to take some swings for an American League produced training video in 1934. The narrator of that video proclaimed Lajoie to be one of the great superstars of yesterday, calling him an "elegant batting specimen who could bring the ball with force to all fields." After watching Napoleon "knock the so called lively ball all over the lot," the commentator asked Lajoie his response to that ball. "Well, if I could start playing all over again," Lajoie responded, "I would never accept a base on balls, and I would never run anything out less than a three bagger." In rare moment of keeping the focus upon himself, he told a reporter that with the lively ball his 1911 home run total of eleven would have been 111. Lajoie didn't hit

*Ty Cobb said that if the Jack Rabbit modern ball had been used
during the Dead Ball Era, Lajoie "would have set records beyond belief."*

11 home runs in 1911 but there is a little truth in what he said, nevertheless.

The American League video provides a unique chance to see how grace and power became bedmates in Lajoie's swing. All of a sudden, calling a swing "elegant" somehow seems an appropriate rather than romanticized description. If only Lajoie's fielding prowess also had been shown in the video. Then, a full appreciation of what Hughes meant when he referred to the "power, rhythm and beauty of action" of Lajoie's play at bat and in the field would have been accomplished. In any case, no other player's hitting style is displayed on the video and no other player is interviewed. It almost seems that the producers felt that

Lajoie's rippling grace deserved to have its final mesmerizing moment on the stage.

Rippling Grace in Motion: Cy Young said of Lajoie,
"He was the Babe Ruth of our time."

Cy Young called Lajoie "the Babe Ruth of our time." Obviously, Lajoie's home run totals were meager compared to the Babe. The average number of home runs per season during the Dead Ball Era was 2.3. Indicative of its insignificance, home run totals were often omitted in player career totals, but stolen bases were not. Lajoie stole 381 bases. Lajoie's greatest seasonal home run production was fourteen, one of the top figures in the DBE. In total, he hit 71 home runs. In 1920, Ruth hit 50 more than any other team in the league. Ruth was a freak. Young made clear the context for his Lajoie-Ruth comparison. Cy and his contemporaries were speaking of prodigious power, not home run production: "Lajoie was one of the most rugged hitters I ever faced. He could take your leg off with a line drive, turn the third baseman around like a swinging door." Not surprisingly, Lajoie often was among the league leaders in doubles and triples. In fact, of his career total of 3200 hits, 641 were doubles.

Upon Lajoie's death in 1959, writers resurrected the question of what Lajoie would have done to the lively ball of today, what feats he might have accomplished if he were not restrained by the "one run at a time" hitting concept of the Dead Ball Era. When yet again asked how many home runs he thought he might have hit, the typically humble Lajoie deferred the question by telling of the hitting exploits of Tiger slugger Sam Crawford. During batting practice Lajoie had watched as Crawford hit dozens of balls out of the park; the motivation for doing so being that youngsters who retrieved and returned them were given free admission to the park. When the game began, however, Crawford would shorten his swing and "go after base hits, any kind, just as the rest of us."

The contention that Lajoie was unfortunate to be born when he was most dramatically developed by sportswriter Joe Williams. Writing in the late 1950's, Williams quoted blond bombshell Jayne Mansfield, "that demure exponent of the mammary school of dramatics," who once admitted that "in the old days, with all those clothes, I'd never have become a star." Similarly, Williams believed that all home run hitters today have to do is bare their muscle. He concluded that "the abundant and arresting form" of the powerfully built Frenchman was concealed by the hitting customs of his time. It was "all a matter of being born at the right time with the right equipment."

Also to be accounted for in any comparative appraisal of Lajoie's power was the murdering of a ball already dead.

Note how far Lajoie choked-up.

CHAPTER EIGHT

Dead On Arrival

It was a spring day in 1906 and the weekly meeting of the Cleveland Ladies Sewing Circle was in full swing. The excited talk was all about baseball and some of the ladies' attention was not focused on their task

"Damn it! That hurts!"

Ignoring the un-lady like cry from a fellow member now sucking the blood out of her pricked dainty finger, the voice from under a hat continued to make her point. "He's a deranged bastard. God knows what he'll do this year."

Chewing a large cud of tobacco, Nellie responded. "Tell you this. I'd love to see Cobb in Cleveland uniform. I'd take him even if he was Jack the Seam Ripper." Gruff laughter filled the room, and Nellie finished her thought. " Imagine him and Nap on the same team."

All needles stopped their work as everyone allowed themselves to envision such a possibility

A stern managerial voice brought an end to their reveries. "Concentrate on your sewing, ladies."

Ignoring the admonition, Nell countered. "Ladies, I could swear I hear a frog croaking. We need to call in an exterminator."

"I'd rather have Eddie Collins anyway," interrupted Georgianna. " Even that big eared squirt would be an improvement over the hayseed we got at second. Don't you agree, ladies?"

There was silence in the room. Only when the stern voiced figure laughed, did the discussion of the proposed Collins trade continue. "Fungo- sticks, Georgianna, you're so silly. Our Nap is so handsome. So tall and muscular. And the way his hair curls down over his forehead. Why he's the D'Artagnan of the Diamond."

A chorus of sighs filled the room.

"Adelaide's right," offered Roberta. "Listen to this." She picked up a newspaper. "The Big Frenchman has a big, finely chiseled nose and a pair of round brown eyes that seem to look right into you." She paused for effect. "and yet they are soft, tender, and gentle." She drew herself up." I mean, ladies, who cares how he plays the game?"

"Mr. Collins is not the gentleman our Napoleon is," Addie added. "He puts his already chewed gum on the crown of his hat until he gets two strikes. Then he puts it in his mouth." Launching a missile of saliva toward a nearby spittoon, she added. "Disgusting."

"I hear that the other day an ump spit in his face. Explained that he didn't like college boys." Another wad of tobacco juice splattered on the floor. " I don't either."

"Mr. Mack got himself a collection of them snobs," grunted Roberta." Suppose that's why our Shoeless Joe had to go. Thanks, Cornelius McGuillicuddy."

Josephina raised her needle as if to acknowledge the compliment but it seems she just needed help from her girlfriends. "Which of you ladies will sew a button on my shirt?"

There was no response and soon the discussion again turned to baseball.

"Why don't we just trade Lajoie for the Big Train? Now, there's a real fastball. I heard that when Chapman was told by Ump Evans that he still had another strike coming, he told him to keep it. He didn't want it."

"I need more emery. The bastards took mine."

"That's what you get for leaving it unattended."

"What are ya, my mother?"

"No, I gave it to yours so her nails look pretty when her boyfriend visits."

"You're a smart ass. Someone ought to..."

"Look, I'm only needling you," Georgianna responded." Get it, you ignorant Mick?"

There was a derisive chorus of gruff laughter. The ladies sewing circle was about to become uncivilized. Fortunately, at this point, a big man walked into the room. "How can a lady sign up for this old maid's club?" he asked.

Taking out a cigar and blowing more foul air into the club-house, the Big Frog croaked his verdict. "Put away your needles and emery boards, ladies. The rookie needs a shower."

A shower of baseball bats swirled by the rookie's head. The meeting was over.

The above conversations and events only bear small resemblance to the actual clubhouse activity that day in Cleveland in 1906. Shoeless Joe Jackson had not yet found his way to Cleveland from Connie Mack's Athletics, and a few liberties have been taken in the characters: Georgina is George Stoval, Josephina is Joe Jackson, and Adelaide is Addie Joss. Of course, the Big Frog is Lajoie. Most of the actual conversation was made up, but according to Lajoie the ball and glove preparations actions were part of a standard ritual. Except for the rookie's provoking comment and the thrown bats to reward him for his effrontery, Nap gave no details on the actual club-house banter. However, players were armed with needles and emery, involved in a standard practice of sewing emery into their gloves, allowing the arriving ball to be scuffed and abraided before it was thrown back to the pitcher, who then worked on loosening the seams. Players who left their gloves unattended on the field between innings would discover that their handwork had been ripped out by opposing players, themselves part of their own sewing circles.

Other acts of chicanery complemented the emery abuse. Since the home team provided the balls, its pitchers took BB pellets and with mallets drove them between the seams of the ball. One pitcher slit the ball with razors along certain seams, providing a great grip. When returning the ball, he would slobber down these elevations with spit and the opposing pitcher and the ump would be unaware of his mutilations. Some pitchers kept nutmeg graters concealed under the fabric in their front pocket. Ever loyal battery mates, catchers gouged the ball against their sharpened belt buckles or the buckles of their catcher's mitts. And, of course, the ball was doctored by various concoctions, including saliva and licorice baths, mud tobacco juice, paraffin rubdowns, and god knows what else. For good measure, the pitcher could stand on the mound and spit on the already abused ball in his hands. The ball was so doctored joked Brooklyn manager Olsen, "that the only thing players didn't do to it was take a bite of it."

Kept in play as long as the frugal umps could justify, distorted, warped, dark, and mushy, the so-called dead ball then had been murdered before it arrived at the plate." We played five or six innings with one ball, and when you connected, it felt as if you had hit a rotten tomato," commented Lajoie. Any wonder then that during the Dead Ball Era (1901-1919), the average batting average was .254 and the average number of home runs hit was 2.3. Of course, the lively ball was on the horizon, a ball Ring Lardner described with disgust as being "so fixed up that if you don't miss it entirely, it will clear the fence."

At 82, Lajoie proclaimed that if he had but one wish it was that "the boys I played with back in 1908 could operate on that jack rabbit ball they are throwing today. Imagine getting a new shiny ball every time you want one."

Ty Cobb selected one player who most would have benefited by the use of that jack rabbit ball. Cobb confidently proclaimed that "Napoleon Lajoie would have set records beyond belief."

CHAPTER NINE

A Big Accident

Writing in the final years of his ninety-one year life span, founding father John Adams made clear his regret that he was not to be a member of a very exclusive club: "No one will ever give me credit. Monuments and mausoleums will never be erected to me. The truth of the history of the American Revolution will never be known. It will be said that Ben Franklin's electric rod smote the earth and up popped George Washington and those two from that point on conducted all military and political affairs by themselves. I care not."

John Adams lied about not caring that he wasn't acknowledged. His correspondence with his wife and with Thomas Jefferson were more than cordialities. Their intention was to make them legacy documents. But before Adams is singled out for undisguised ego, it is only fair to add another Founding Father to the list of legacy hounds. George Washington petitioned and received from the Continental Congress money to hire ten secretaries to capture his correspondence and notes. All this at a time when the Continental Army was ill-fed and underequipped. At least, Thomas Jefferson used his own funds to create a machine that copied for posterity his ideas and correspondences.

The Founding Fathers then had a righteousness about them, a sense that they merited lasting recognition. Of course, they did, and citizens and historians arewe are all thankful for their actions. Meanwhile, one of the founding fathers of the American League, frugal Napoleon Lajoie bought himself four speckled black and white composition books and over the years meticulously cut and pasted articles about himself, a scrapbook meant to be savored over the years and shared with intimate friends.

Adams' perceived sense of injustice has been somewhat rectified by a popular television mini-series and a best-selling biography. In addition, in Braintree, MA, pedestrians walk past an impressive enough statue of their native son. The fact is though that Adams will never be in the three-man pantheon of Franklin, Jefferson and Washington. That's the way it is.

Napoleon Lajoie knew that was the way it was. During and after his career, the electric rods of Ty Cobb and Babe Ruth conducted the baseball affairs of the country. Their magnetic personalities and electrifying performances on the field enthralled a nation. Ruth and Cobb were attention seeking missiles who provided continuous copy for legions of sportswriters. The baseball propaganda machine found a way to capitalize on everything they did, chastising or covering up their excesses while parading their achievements and courting their attention. Until their deaths, neither of the men was willing to move out of that limelight.

Lajoie admitted that he liked "the attention as much as the other guy," and later in his career he spoke modestly of his importance in establishing the credibility of the nascent American League, even suggesting that if he had failed to produce on the field as he had during that 1901 season, the league might have been disbanded. He also acknowledged his ground breaking defiance of the reserve clause and its importance to the rights of players that followed. Yet, unlike Cobb and Adams and Jefferson and Washington, Lajoie was not tethered to a legacy building agenda.

No doubt, he saw fame as having a dark lining: "I bought a chicken farm out east to be alone but no! Might as well hang out at second base. The farmers point out my house. The conductors call it out as if it were a train station. Newspaper photographers come out and photo me, Mrs. Lajoie, the pigs, the chickens. Darn soon the horses will be asking for agents and the chickens will refuse to lay eggs until they get a movie contract."

Lajoie did not beat around the bush when it came to his distaste of public scrutiny and press excesses: "I don't like this. I never have, never will. Yeah, I like to hear nice things said about me, but enough is enough. Sometimes I wish I could keep out of the limelight. I'd have more peace of mind if they'd let me alone with my hack driving down in Woonsocket, RI...I go to town to buy #80 black sewing cotton for my wife and all I hear is 'There goes Lajoie.' I go to a show with my wife and all we hear is 'There's Lajoie.' It's embarrassing, and I don't enjoy the show."

During one interview, Lajoie's disgust at the press's invasion of his private life exploded in a tirade aimed at the paparazzi of his time: "Okay, you want more? I was born on September 5, 1875 in Woonsocket, RI. I have three gold fillings. I weigh 196 pounds and am 6 feet, 1 inch. I like buttermilk. Yes, I like Ty Cobb. The farm is 12 miles outside of Cleveland. Mrs. Lajoie uses a cross stitch to darn my socks. My hens lay 16 eggs a day."

Larry with one of his prize-wining roosters.
"Come winter, you'll find Old Larry right there," he said of the farm.

Larry ended the tirade with biting sarcasm: "Bye now. Come back when you a late for the train!"

Especially during his playing days, he did not want the press to believe for a moment that they had seduced him with their litany of praise. "Sometimes when I have been reading this or that about this big mutt Lajoie. I feel like going down to the back lot, digging a hole, jumping in and pulling the hole in after me. No, you don't believe me; you've been reading your own stuff so long that you have a sneaking suspicion that I memorize it and have it set to music."

Despite his avoidance of the limelight, Nap was not a recluse. He was more comfortable being the host than the visitor. His home was never off limits. Writers and ballplayers and fans came to visit him, both on the farm in Cleveland and at his Florida retirement homes. Chris Mathewson and Chief Meyers visited the farm. National journalists such as Jimmy Powers and Arthur Daley made frequent stops. And, of course, small time New England scribes were welcomed. One such writer, Frank McGrath, was invited back every year for five years, an open invitation McGrath thought was due to his Fall River roots. "Lajoie loved to discuss the Fall River he remembered. He never failed to talk about Artie Butler, former major leaguer from Fall River, and the Herald News."

Folks from Woonsocket and environs had only to ask to visit and were ushered into Poli's presence- a Good Neighbor Open Door Policy of sorts. One Woonsocket resident recalled with fondness his 1956 visit with his wife to Lajoie's home, part of their honeymoon trip. Lajoie was 80 years old at the time. The couple spent four hours at the home, and came back the next day. An autographed Lajoie ball is his proudest possession.

Those who had proven their friendship need not have had a Woonsocket pedigree. The owner Charles Marston, the owner of the

Fall River Indians, Lajoie's first professional team, remained a life-long friend. Cleveland Mayor Johnson was another close friend. Upon his deathbed, he wished Lajoie and the Naps well in the coming season. Pugilists, clerks, millionaires, all formed part of a small egalitarian circle.

Lajoie then was hardly anti-social. He liked his social life in small doses. He liked to play poker once a week with a bunch of newsman and fellow players. In Woonsocket, in Cleveland, on the train with teammates, among golf fellows who greeted him with "Hey, Nap" when he entered the clubhouse. A close friend clarified the misconception that Lajoie was snobbish. "He's not a good mixer. He doesn't take up with people on first meeting, but gain his friendship and he is loyal to a fault." In other words, he brought a small town provincial mentality easily made uncomfortable with new situations, large numbers, and new expectations. This could be misunderstood, as when he was accused of only inviting a small number of friends to an event. A friend came to Lajoie's defense: "There's no folk like the old folk. Down in Woonsocket they weren't so fickle. They didn't say that "The King" didn't know how to play baseball because he asked friends to eat crabs with him, instead of inviting the whole town to a clambake." According to the writer, "the folks in Woonsocket remember when the King of the Diamond was a chambermaid in a livery stable. They were the first ones to see traces of conceit, if he had any."

One paper offered its explanation of Lajoie's' social reticence. "He was a bashful kid who had the traits of his race… You know them, those natives of New France… the Rhode Island Lajoies drifted down towards the factory towns of the south from Quebec. The size of the family indicates that they were descended from those habitant families who gave every twelfth child to the church, and usually made contributions of two children."

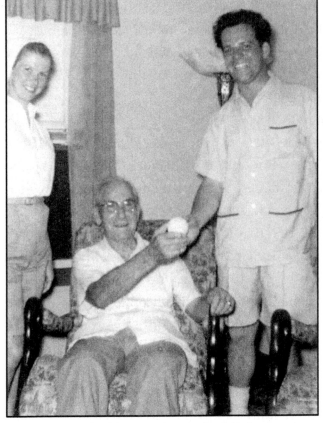

A newlywed Woonsocket couple visits Larry.
They were invited to come back the next day, and they did.

Lajoie did love his farm. As he proclaimed, "Come winter, you'll find old Larry right there." Lajoie explained that as a youth he had been influenced "by the return to the farm" movement that offered a return to clearer moral values and the open space of nature to develop them. It might not have always been so quiet on that farm, however. The story goes that when the moon arose, neighbors for miles around had to close their windows to shut out the howls of Lajoie's hounds. Dressed in farmer overalls, he raised geese, pigs, and chicken. He cleaned the horse stalls and the chicken coops. The rest of the farm family? A dog named Mike who guarded the family despite having lost a few teeth playing catch, and Polly and Molly, two beloved horses who earned their keep by pulling the plough. So embraced were Polly and Molly and Mike that photos of them are included in Lajoie's scrapbooks.

Mike and Polly and Molly were too smart to think that their owner would ever abandoned baseball for them. Baseball was and would always be his bloodline. Even in the early years of his baseball career, he capitalized upon his fame by organizing barnstorming teams, coming to Woonsocket often and across the country as well. In 1921, he attended an Indians' Old Timers game and at 46 was the only old-timer to play the entire game. In 1957, he threw out the first pitch for a Giants-Cleveland exhibition. Earlier, he had attended a game that resulted in Cleveland capturing the pennant. Since Lajoie had never won a pennant during his career in major league baseball, it must have been a more than a bittersweet moment, but he went. All in all, as his "disappearance" before the Cooperstown induction confirms, Larry Lajoie preferred to stay at home, keep a low profile.

Of course, he attended the Cooperstown induction ceremony in June of 1939. His speech was short and sweet: "Ladies and gentlemen, I am very glad to be here today and meet the old-timers which many of you have watched playing baseball and some of the greatest men who have ever walked on the ball field, and I am glad to have the honor of joining them. I hope everyone enjoys it as much as I do." After meeting the fans and enjoying a dinner with the players, he quickly headed back home.

No doubt Lajoie received many invitations to attend events at various venues but as he acknowledged in a 1953 letter to Cooperstown historian Ernest Lanigan, Mrs. Lajoie's health was an impediment. "I get an invitation from Cooperstown every year but have to pass it up on account of her condition." In point of fact, Mrs. Lajoie bears too much accountability for Larry's reluctance to attend events. His niece told the story of an older Lajoie, now living with her in Daytona following Mrs. Lajoie's death. It seemed that Larry got off the phone after declining an invitation from fellow HOF'er Tris Speaker to come to the Indians spring training facility nearby. The plan was to honor Larry with a special day. Although his health was fine, Lajoie had politely declined the invite.

"Uncle Larry, why not?" I said to him. "They want to honor you. They love you. Why not accept, and we will all go out there and have a good time."

Like an embarrassed child, a reluctant Nap had his niece call Speaker back. She was glad she had provoked her uncle to go. "They advertised about Larry and a good crowd was there." Pressured by her to buy a new grey suit and new hat for the occasion, "Uncle Larry looked handsome-still tall and straight at 82. After the game there was a reception at Indianville. Everybody had a great time. Then around seven that evening, my husband and I had another party for him and had dinner. There were about 80 there. When we got home that evening, he was tired but so happy. We talked about the game and party for weeks."

This did not mean that henceforth Larry in old age became a gad-fly eager to enjoy last hurrahs. A year later, a year before his death, he was spied one afternoon standing beyond the centerfield fence watching Little Leaguers play. An official asked him to at least allow himself to be introduced, after all he was the honorary president of the Daytona Little League. Lajoie declined. "No, no, please. Let some of the younger men take a bow."

Lajoie signing autographs at his Cooperstown induction.

Since it was all a matter of luck, there was no need to get a swelled head, no need to make too much of all or any of this. "I sometimes feel glad that there aren't any young Lajoies. A kid's head is turned so easily…give a kid a lot of hero worship because his pa is a poor sucker who doesn't know anything but baseball, and he's apt to become all swelled up. I'd take half my time paddling the ego out of a Johnny Lajoie, and I'd spent the rest trying to keep my marriage together."

Lajoie knew the ride would end. "I know I'm a drawing card. I know I am a public figure," he revealed." But I won't always be a public figure, always a drawing card, so I have been striving ever since I came into notice as a baseball player to keep it from turning my head." Let others suffer the maladjustment they had invited by self-decep tion; he had worked too hard to be duped or used by anyone. And he wasn't about to be seduced by a trap set by the mistress called fame.

"The piercing and blinding limelight of public idolatry is too much for some men. This is not true of Lajoie for he is still in possession of his senses. It is no small matter to withstand its grip. It makes paupers of a few, drunkards of a few, and fools of many." Written about Lajoie during the peak of his popularity in Cleveland, Archie Bell's assessment of Lajoie was on target.

"Still in possession of his senses," Lajoie also wasn't going to be foolish enough to fall into the trap of thinking that he had been pre-ordained for a blessed life, a tempting seduction for a mill kid thinking he had escaped the grinding belt and spewing smokestacks forever. "I never lose sight of the fact that I may be a dead one in a baseball way tomorrow," he told a reporter. Interviewed in *American Boy* (1908) magazine, Lajoie told youngsters seeking a baseball career to "…play with all your heart and soul," but at the same time" build a foundation for afterlife." Lajoie worked as hard as any to keep in shape because he understood that lucky or not, he had to get the most out of the gift given, driven by not only by pride but by a wariness that all could collapse suddenly. Players reported that Lajoie was often the last one to leave the ballpark. After fifteen years, the regiment held true-twenty times round the bases, twenty minutes of "fast fielding." The 3'S's he professed to living by- savings, system, and stick-to-itive-ness- were also part of a belief that what you held in your hand today could be gone tomorrow. So make hay while you can, keep in position to capitalize if opportunity knocks. "A ball player's success in life after years on the diamond depends what he does with his leisure hours during his days as a player," Lajoie declared. Invest in that cigar store, publish those baseball guides, take a job while in Woonsocket visiting.

Retiring in comfort, he continued to follow opportunities given, from tire salesman to minor league manager.

Unplugging a writer's string of compliments about him, Lajoie declared," Look, I'm not a poem turned to flesh and blood. I'm just a big accident, just as lucky as when my cab horse ran away back in Woonsocket and just missed a cop." There was great humility in this "poor sucker," but his "don't make too much of all this" attitude was a way of keeping himself grounded.

Again, Mr. Lajoie was on the other side of the street from Mr. Cobb.

One of many examples of Lajoie's work ethic.

CHAPTER TEN

Don't Make Too Much Out of Any of This

S cience was all the rage at the turn of the century. Now a major industrial power, America touted its scientific prowess and embraced the belief that scientific advancement was the pathway to societal progress. After all, the Wright Brothers had just taken to the sky and sent aloft dreams of the possibilities. Car sales were booming and motion pictures were creating new realities for entranced audiences. Americans dropped the pitchfork and grabbed the phone. They also attended The *Meet Me in St Louie, Louie* 1904 World's Fair, intended to be a celebration of America's dedication to science. There were other triumphs to be celebrated. In the first American hosted Olympics, the United States won 238 of the total 282 medals awarded, seen as a testimony to America virtues of athleticism, intelligence, and resolve. In reality, only 13 countries sent teams and 533 of the total 625 participants were Americans; travel and the on-going Russo-Japanese War discouraged foreign participant.

Ty Cobb considered baseball a science and himself to be a man of science. Later in life, he made clear that if he had not chosen baseball as a career, he would have chosen medicine. He prided himself on studying the game in all its facets. In fact, he did not consider the game as it was later played as even being baseball. "They don't play baseball anymore," he declared in a Life Magazine article in 1952. "Science is out the window." As to himself, Cobb declared that he had so studied hitting, so employed the scientific approach to its secrets, that he "knew everything there was to know about it." When asked who was the ball player's ball player of all time, Cobb picked Eddie Collins because Collins could play "inside and brainy baseball." Ironically, both men of science by their spectacular style of play rescued the game from being dominated by passionless scientific application, as in the case of a St Louis manager who ordered 15 consecutive bunts

Lajoie agreed with Cobb's teammate Sam Crawford that the basis of Cobb's superiority was that he "out thought everyone." Lajoie identified a particular of Cobb's genius. "Ty was a man who took advantage of every psychological factor. As a ballplayer he was no better than any of the rest, except perhaps for his legs. The thing that made him great was his ability to make a keen analysis of any situation, pick out a weak spot and play to that spot. He used the other man's jitters to his own advantage."

Lajoie also appreciated Cobb's committed study of all phases of the game. He recalled that Cobb's preparatory pre-game rituals included practicing how he would launch his many slides, each time changing the angle of his slide and the distance of his slide from the bag. The whole thing was a scientific experiment of sorts. "Meanwhile, he was covered in bruises," said Lajoie, with clear admiration more for the discipline and passion that ignored pain.

Cobb would not have been pleased to hear himself introduced in the Hall of Fame Induction ceremony as the player "who won the hearts of fans by playing the brand of ball called daring, reckless, and devil-may-care." Ty would have no trouble with being described as daring for that was a manly attribute, but he was far too calculating and analytical to be called reckless and devil-may-care. Of course, all this is moot since Cobb missed the Hall of Fame Induction ceremony. Either he had a touch of ptomaine poisoning or he missed travel connections, or he was symbolically protesting against his nemesis Commissioner Kenesaw Landis, but for whatever reason, he again had created controversy and put himself in the limelight.

Cobb would also have vehemently rejected being called a natural hitter, for in Cobb's mind such a hitter lacked application and knowledge. He argued that such players, especially Joe Jackson, sadly had limited their potential by playing without such a scientific approach. Lajoie was introduced that Cooperstown afternoon as a "great natural hitter." He had no problem with that designation. Having watched Lajoie play for over ten years at Cleveland, Grantland Rice spoke of his amazing intuition-the best in baseball. "None of us could ever see that he was trying to do any thinking or trying to make plays in advance." Lajoie, he contended, "had a genius of instinct. He knew." It is reasonable to conclude then that everything Lajoie did just came naturally, that his nonchalance and his seemingly effortless performances at the plate and in the field, meant that he needn't have to be a student of the game. In fact, he wasn't. If there were those who extolled the virtues of scientific study of the game and explained the logic behind their hitting, fielding, and running style, Lajoie was not one of them.

Lajoie, in fact, seemed to relish debunking ideas that baseball was a marriage of science and skill: "Baseball is more of a trade than a science. Did a boilermaker ever take you aside and in a few well-chosen words tell you how to make boilers? Well, it's the same with baseball. Luck and nature do more than anything else towards making a ball player."

Lajoie also mocked the idea that he was seer. When the questioner persisted in trying to get Lajoie to declare baseball a cerebral activity, a thinking man's game, he responded, "This is the way it goes. I go up and hit the ball." "When a man is eating, he doesn't have to stop as he does to ask himself 'How high should I hold the fork at every bit or how wide should I open my mouth?'"

Neither was baseball a cat and mouse game between the hitter and the pitcher. "Outguess the pitcher? I never try. The pitcher's thoughts are his own.... I don't know what he is thinking about, and I don't care... It doesn't matter to me whether he throws a curve or a fast one as long as he gets it over the plate."

Confirmation of Lajoie's approach came from Hall of Famer Jack Chesbro. Chesbro was asked by a rookie about to face Lajoie what he should throw him. "He has no preferences," responded Chesbro. When the rookie persisted, asking what he should pitch to get him out, Chesbro reported his strategy when facing Lajoie. "I put everything I have on the ball and then trust that nothing serious happens. If he makes an out, I am thankful. If he makes a single, I am pleased that he didn't hit a double. If he hits a double, I am pleased that he didn't hit a triple. If he hits a triple, I feel it could have been worst." Umpire Bill Evans, sitting on the bench at the time, recalls that Chesbro stood up and delivered his final advice to the rook: "The less serious you take Larry, the more successful you probably will be." Perhaps Chesbro should have simply told the rookie to take the bat out of Lajoie's hand, as Chesbro himself once did when he hit Lajoie three times and walked him on his fourth and final at bat.

All this is not to say that Lajoie didn't have a fierce concentration when hitting. He may have approached the box with nonchalance, and he may have held the bat with ease in his left hand as he stood to bat, but Lajoie knew he had work to do. "I never take my eye off the pitcher's hand, and I try not to be deceived by the revolutions of the windup. When the ball comes in, I judge it as carefully as I can and swing to meet it."

Lajoie's batting position reflected his resolve that batting was not a game of adjustments. Even if the pitcher was painting the outside corner with his fastball or throwing that sweeping curve that kissed the outside corner, there was no need to move closer to the plate. Hall of Famer Ed Walsh, who considered Lajoie the greatest hitter he ever faced, said that Lajoie "never broke ground." He explains: "No matter where I pitched the ball, he was always in the same spot on the next pitched ball." Amazingly, Lajoie was only beaned once in his career. That does not mean that he wasn't thrown at often, including the high and hard one near the head. Connie Mack couldn't recall a single instance when Lajoie fell to the ground to avoid being hit. Pitcher Lena Blackburne, who played often against

Lajoie agreed, adding that he had asked of many who played against Lajoie if he could recall such an instance. "I have yet to find any-one.... that's a wonderful tribute to his eyes," he said with amazed admiration.

In a game that speaks constantly of the necessity that batters make adjustments if they are to survive, Lajoie was an anomaly. One manager of a rival team recalled that there was glee in his clubhouse when one of his pitchers struck Lajoie out twice in the same game and did not come close to anything resembling a hit. His secret seemed to be a high hard one thrown near his head. With such a "way to pitch Lajoie" finally having been discovered, the manager, Hall of Famer Hugh Duffy, gave direction to the next day pitcher to continue the magic elixir. Accordingly, the first pitch thrown to Lajoie that day was a pitch up at his neck. Lajoie slammed it over the left field fence. Feeling no need to be discouraged, Duffy ordered another high hard one targeted for the neck. Lajoie hit the pitch so hard that it caromed off the brick outfield wall and traveled back to within ten feet of the infield. Lajoie only got a double. After another hit proved that three was not a charm, the decision was made to abandon the plan. Lajoie followed with two more hits. Not surprisingly, Duffy made it clear that "the grand Larry" would the first player he would select for his team would be Lajoie, "even if he had but one arm." To explain the armless reference, he told of the greatest feat he had ever seen in the majors- After passing on first two pitches that were each a foot out-side, Lajoie reached out with only one hand on the bat to hit the next offering, also way outside. The ball traveled over the centerfield fence.

Part of Lajoie's intractability might have been that the stub-born Frenchman was unwilling to concede that the opposition had proven a way to best him. More likely, though, Blackburne's assessment was on target- he had a great pair of eyes. Ty Cobb, in fact, admitted that Lajoie had a better eye than he did. He may have swung at any pitches he could reach, including waste pitches, but he knew exactly how far outside or inside they were. Players today speak of the importance of knowing where the pitch was, Lajoie knew exactly where it was. In explaining the mystery of how he could hit a ball no matter where it was pitched, he responded, "It was all in the eyes, which saw at once where the ball was going and sent the message to the arm and hands." He mentioned to writers that players worried too much about the legs and not enough about taking care of the eyes. Rather than building the discipline of not swinging at bad pitches, every spring Lajoie practiced hitting the ball no matter where it was thrown. God-given gifts were to be preserved and refined, not taken for granted.

As a ball player, he did not abuse himself with worry and expectation. No self-doubt entered the picture when he went hitless. "When I hit it right, I am not unlucky enough to aim it directly at a fielder, I get a safe hit. If I don't, I lose. That's all there is to hitting and no one can tell me more there is more to it than that."" Not surprisingly, Larry did not take coaching on hitting well, especially it came from junior players who had the audacity to try to instruct him.

And what about slumps? Cobb solution was to practice harder, focusing that practice on putting the ball in play, cutting down on his swing to hit the ball back to the pitcher or some designated hard to reach spot for fielders. Of course, bunting might be part of the thinking man's strategy to overcome his dilemma. Lajoie didn't believe in slumps. This is not to say he didn't practice certain swing techniques nor that he didn't believe in conditioning to be keep prepared. He may have been alert for bad habits but, for Lajoie, willing to concede that success or failure came as a result of luck as well as capability, slumps per se didn't exist: . "Here is the way it goes. I go up and hit the ball. The fielder goes after it. He just gets it and I am out. Back to the bench for me. I go up again. I hit the ball hard. Same thing. That man in center goes crazy with the heat. Runs three miles, Jumps twelve feet in the air and catches it on his thumb. I get that handed to me for two or three days and the people, begin to ask, 'What's the matter with Larry?' Now, I am hitting the ball just as hard as ever, but the luck of the game is against me. That's all. The next day, I go up and swat it, and some guy runs under it too far, and I get around to second. And the fans proclaim, 'Larry's got his batting eye back!' Then again I walk up to the plate. I get my eye on the ball and paste it hard. It sails out on a line and the fielder going after it finds his arm a half-inch too short. The ball keeps rolling, and Larry gets credit for it. Great batter! Now if that infielder had not stood so close to himself, and had grown a half inch more of arm, the side would have been retired, and everyone would have said, 'That bone-head hit right into someone's hands.' That's baseball for you. It's the luck of the game."

That luck could be fickle. It may have given Lajoie the singles and doubles and triples, but when it came to having the one thing he wanted more than anything else, the chance to play in a World Series, it turned its back. During his entire major league career, Lajoie never won a pennant. Reviews of Lajoie's baseball achievements invariably mention this fruitless part of his career and the *King without a Crown* descriptions began as early as five years into his Cleveland tenure. Two seasons in particular remained open wounds for Lajoie through-out his life. In the 1905 season, with the team coasting in first place, Lajoie was spiked and suffered infections so serious that doctors spoke of amputation. He came to home games in a wheelchair and never returned to the field that season. Without their star, the team went quietly into the night. The spiking was the impetus for using white sanitary socks that covered ankles and calves under color pigmented socks with stirrups. Bloody socks may be hung in the trophy case with care, as were Curt Schillings' bloody white socks at the Hall of Fame, but without the trophy, there is no display.

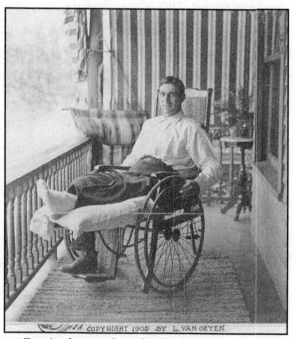

Good News: Despite doctor's fears that his leg may have to be amputated, Lajoie recovered from blood poisoning after being spiked. Bad News: Another pennant-promising season was lost.

In 1908, the team came within a half a game of winning the pennant. Down the stretch, poor umpire calls and key failures by usually reliable players, including himself, made the difference and Ty Cobb's Tigers advanced to the World Series. Four years before his death, Lajoie said that he would have given half a dozen years of his life to have won that pennant. He admitted that he had joined Connie

Mack's A's for two final seasons in the hope that their magic might rub off on him. Lajoie was then over forty. Like so many athletes in whatever sport, a crown without the jewel of post season appearance and success lacked that special shine.

During a Cooperstown interview, Lajoie tempered his excitement for the game with a sobering qualification that no doubt was born of his own deep regret. "It's a wonderful game," he told sportswriter Jimmy Powers, "but you have to have the luck and the breaks." In the later years of Lajoie's career, some writers referred to him as jinxed. You get the feeling that he might have agreed with them.

The ad was in color.
Lajoie was the first athlete to be featured in a colored ad.

CHAPTER ELEVEN

Social Drama

As future Hall of Famer second baseman Eddie Collins stepped into the batter's box, Umpire Laughlin spit on him. Asked afterward why he had done so, Laughlin responded, "I don't like college boys." His answer made clear it wasn't anything personal. He and Collins had no personal history of disagreements or confrontations. Might it have been a symbolic act? A social class action suit on behalf of the street urchins upset that Miss Hamilton Marshal-Gray 's silver spooned kids were the ones trespassing. The game on the professional level had never been the game of Mr. Cartwright and his fellow gentlemen playing on Elysian Field fifty years ago. It was the game of men whose roots were in the macadam of the street or the dirt of the backyard or field, men who worked in the grime of the mill, had walked in pig and chicken and cow excrement, worked and worked some more. Perhaps Laughlin's spit was a moist backlash at the perceived haughtiness of these college boys.

From 1900 to 1910, the United States population grew by 8 million, the majority of that growth an immigrant swarm, with the majority of that swarm settling in the bee hive urban world of the northeast. With teams in these cities, baseball could call itself a call to all, from accountant to farm boy to millworker. However, at the professional level at this time it was in reality a vocation for the poor. At the turn of the century, the grand majority of the players who were in the profession leagues were poorly educated and came from the lower economic class. Hugh Duffy was a dye shirt worker. Big Ed Walsh and Honus Wagner, coalminers. Cap Anson and Cy Young, farmers. Walter Johnson and Cleveland Alexander, telephone linemen. Tris Speaker, bronco buster. And so forth. Since blacks were excluded, other lower level income populations filled the gap, with "Shanty" Irish players most prominent filling the rosters.

Of course, Laughlin's actions did nothing but confirm baseball's own propagandist contention that such educated types as Collins were indeed superior in demeanor to the men they replaced. Indeed, *Baseball Magazine* proudly proclaimed in 1911 that "the typical baseball player was now a gentleman in all ways, a growing percentage college educated and fitted for higher professions." Non-educated players must have bristled upon reading that "ladies could now ask their escorts to take them to the Polo Grounds to see the college boys play." What were they, chopped liver? Wasn't the player considered by his peers to be the gentleman of gentlemen, Addie Joss, the son of a cheesemaker?

Ironically, a man who was once a member of their fraternity, a shoemaker, would lead the way in bringing the college men aboard. Eddie Collins was but one of a number of college educated teammates recruited by Connie Mack to represent his faith in their transformative potential. Mack's 1910 Athletics, that of the "100,000 Infield," were the most highly educated team in baseball history. Illiterate Joe Jackson was jettisoned from the team and ended up joining forces with the boy from the mills, Lajoie.

In any regard, Neanderthals had been shown the exit. If baseball had earlier taken stern measures to curb its rowdyism, player and fan alike, it now looked to college boys to carry their pedigree across the white lines and help make baseball entertainment suitable for moms and the family, for guys and their dates. A song written by George Cohen in the same year as "Take Me Out to the Ballgame," made clear that such ballpark dates would be stimulating in a different way. The girl of the time rejected the "sweetest of tunes sung by her beloved." Instead, she demanded to go to the game for "I like to get the crowd going and root and hoot and shout. I want to go to the pastime, have a fast time like the last time."

Napoleon Lajoie's portrayal in that 1907 colored Coke advertisement is instructive in distinguishing Lajoie's reputation as a player. In the ad, Nap strolls towards a family enjoying the atmosphere at the ball park. Dressed in her widow's hat, a wife prepares to sip on Coke as her children and husband surround her. The ad is a tamed family version of Cohen's dating scene. She seems far too refined to hoot and holler and shout. The ad, however, confirms that

Lajoie was part of the solution, not the problem. Families could feel comfortable and secure, and ladies could privately swoon as the handsome Lajoie paraded about. Coke had done their homework, listened to the reviews. Lajoie was a man of integrity whose solid work habits and sound morals were a far cry from the boisterous buffoonery and dissolution associated with past players arising from the unwashed. Although he was one of many such decent types, Lajoie was singled out by many. One baseball historian claimed that "... no player was more successful in enhancing professional baseball's public respectability."

Even as the point was that gentleman need not have a pedigree, social class prejudice was hard to shake. "Lajoie failed to obtain the education of most of his fellows," said journalist Sam Crane, "and was a very crude young man at first but being quick witted and observing and having the rough edges of manners rounded by travel and association with people, became gentlemanly and polished." Although Crane's remarks were well intentioned, Lajoie might have found the explanation lacking; certainly, his "unpolished" friends in Woonsocket who shared his realities growing up and rarely left their circle of friends nor traveled, were respected by Poli.

In reality, Napoleon Lajoie harbored no overriding resentment of the college boys. He had admiration for Collins, who played the game with the spunk and hardnosed aggressiveness he admired. He entertained on his farm the poster boy of the college educated gentleman, Christy Mathewson, playing catch with eggs. Of course, he did remind Christy that these eggs were the equivalent of diamonds to country folk.

Lajoie's actual discovery was embedded in social class drama, nevertheless. On July 4, 1895, Lajoie's "Woonsockets" team played the Carters of Franklin, Massachusetts. The pitcher that day

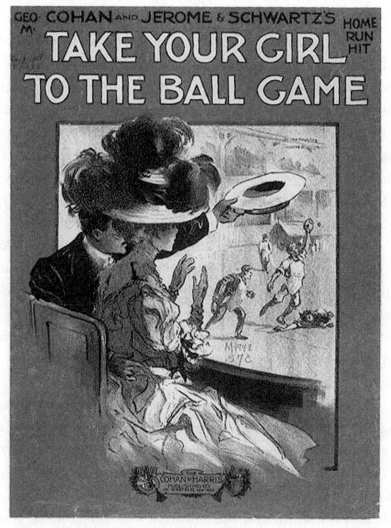

"I like to get the crowd going and hoot and shout. I want to go to the pastime, have a fast time like last time." – From the Library of Congress Collection on Internet Sheet Music.

was Fred Woodcock, a Brown University hurler. Lajoie's recollection of the day reveals there was social tension in the air: "He came to play us, with a lot of other fresh college fellows. I was a joke to him, I guess. I know he was a joke to me. Not as a pitcher but because of the loud clothes he wore." For his part, Woodcock made light fun of Lajoie's unpolished demeanor and his appearance. In words that echoed Hapgood's earlier description of Lajoie, he described Lajoie as a primitive type from the hinterlands, especially noting his old glove and his out of style and worn canvas sneakers that he guessed would soon be discarded. Ironically, those canvas sneakers would be carried to Fall River and kept as keepsakes as he traveling from hotel to hotel during his professional career. Reminders of how far he had come? Superstitious good luck charms? Symbols of his social allegiance and roots? Probably all three.

Apart from his apparel and demeanor observations, Woodcock spoke with awe of Lajoie's exploits at bat. "I couldn't even get a ball past the raw Frenchman. No matter how high or low, wide or close," contended Woodcock, "he simply stepped into 'em and killed 'em. He hit one clear over the back fence and into the river and there was another that I think never hit any place and is still going."

Lajoie was less histrionic in his account, but he admitted to being on a roll that day. "I had my batting eye that day, and I hit 'em every time up." He recalled that Woodcock was "so fired mad that the last time I was up he pegged it straight at my head. To save the Lajoie bean, I dodged. As I dodged, I took a poke at the ball, just for luck. It connected and the ball went over the fence. It was an accident if there ever was one." Depending on what account you buy into, Woodcock either was in awe or was one peeved college kid. Despite attributing his homer to a lucky swing, Lajoie clearly felt he has schooled the college pitcher. Lajoie elsewhere commented that "the college pitcher passed on the story of the merciless slugger from Woonsocket to the manager of the Boston National who was interested in the Woonsocket cab driver who had knocked his friend all over the field. But he had heard of phenoms before and refused to pay carfare down to Woonsocket to see me perform." Defending his unresponsiveness, owner Selee later explained that "there isn't a village in New England that hasn't sent me word to come over and look at *Jake the World Beater* or *Little Bill the Wizard.*"

It was Woodcock who got the ball rolling, asking Lajoie if he was interested in playing for the Carters. Lajoie's famous six-word response, "I am all out for the stuff," said it all. Throughout his life, Lajoie always guarded his "stuff" carefully and considered frugality an important virtue. He also used it as motivation, telling one outfielder to think of a fly ball as a dollar bill to be collected. Woodcock soon afterward contacted the manager of the Fall River team, Charles Marston. "You ought to go over and have a look at a Big Frenchy they got on the Woonsocket team," Woodcock implored. Marston did venture to Woonsocket, although not primarily to see Lajoie but to visit his aunt. Before that visit with Marston was over, Lajoie had committed to a one hundred dollar a month contract to play for Fall River. The story persists that Marston forgot to bring a contract and so Lajoie signed on an envelope. It would have been in character for Lajoie to honor such a deal no matter. The two remained friends for life, with each frequently taking of the integrity of the other. Later, Marston would give the sentimental Lajoie the actual contract that he signed to play for the Fall River Indians. Lajoie also tracked down a team photo of Fall River team as a keepsake.

Marston knew what he had in Lajoie, of course. When he sold Lajoie to Philadelphia, he issued an assurance. "You are paying $1,500 for a player you would not sell for $10,000 after one season with you." The Phillies didn't have to be told about Lajoie's potential. Their scout had run to the telegraph office to wire his report: "This Lajoie is a find. He will be the grandest player of them all."

Back to the Woodcock-Lajoie affair. Both Woodcock's and Lajoie's accounts of their confrontation in Woonsocket are stretches, although Lajoie's home run acrobatics jive with accounts by Hall of Fame pitchers Chesbro and Walsh and others who marveled at his ability to hit unhittable pitches and to administer revenge for bean ball tactics. What is more remarkable is that baseball historians can only unearth two box scores in which Lajoie faced Woodcock. He was hitless in both.

Perhaps then this was another game, unrecorded for some reason. No matter what, each man's memory was a servant to mythologies. For Woodcock, the narrative was part of a frequently told and massaged tale that confirmed him as the discerning one who discovered the Emperor of the Baseball Diamond, even as he added to the lore of Lajoie's amazing power at the plate. To Lajoie, the game represented a lesson delivered to a snobbish member of a supposedly superior fraternity. Since Woodcock and he shared no past antagonistic history of words or confrontations, there was nothing personal going on. Significantly, in neither account does Lajoie identify Woodcock by name, he was "the college pitcher" among "other fresh college fellows." In other words, a member of a fraternity of judgmental brats to whom he was a joke. Lajoie didn't spit in the face of "the college boy" like Umpire Laughlin, but he delivered a message of how little he thought of him. He did not appreciate being looked down upon anyone, especially by those who had been handed everything and risked little. Napoleon was proud of his roots. He needed to apologize to no one. In fact, he understood that he was championed by many who shared his humble beginnings.

"The glory of France and Woonsocket,
Lajoie is the greatest hitter of them all.
The greatest batsman that ever knocked
the eternal epidermis off the ball."

Grantland Rice

CHAPTER TWELVE

A Tale of Three Cities and Then Some

On September 15, 1903, as a member of the Cleveland Indians, Napoleon Lajoie came to Fall River to play an exhibition game. No doubt he was anxious for the city had declared the date to be "Lajoie Day." However comfortable and talented in playing the game, he was never comfortable with adulation nor with ceremonial talk. They were plenty of both awaiting him.

Despite the fact that it was work day, fans streamed to the game. Baseball historian James Murphy recounted the game day drama of what he called "the most memorable day in the city's sports history":

> *People left their posts in the mills. Housewives baked early and they and their young ones came, too. Game time was mid-afternoon. The bleachers were filled before noon. The grandstand was almost filled an hour and a half before the first pitch.... The horse gate on Oak Grove Avenue never handled so much traffic. Kids sat on the top of the fence, angering other non-payers whose views from nearby trees they obstructed.*

The cover of a 1990 edition of Sports Collector's Digest *paraded Lajoie's Rhode Island roots.*

Standing before an embarrassed Lajoie, Mayor Grimes got to the point of the celebration of Lajoie Day. "Your success has demonstrated to our youth, "he proclaimed, "that earnest endeavor and diligence will receive its special reward." Those enterprising kids sitting atop the fence heard the message free and clear. Politician Grimes ended his remarks by reminding all that Napoleon had begun his professional career playing for the 1896 Fall River Indians. "It is a special honor that the Fall River Club has furnished the baseball firmament the greatest and brightest star that has appeared in its galaxy."

The Mayor's appraisal of Lajoie's talent and national reputation was not parochial bias. Of course there was the extraordinary 1901 season, but the year before that he had hit .346, and the year afterward, he hit .366. Lajoie was an entrenched star.

Most of those who attended the game had followed the Big Frenchman since his playing days with the Fall River Indians. Lajoie remembered that his first steps onto the Dexter Street Grounds were not his fondest. His straw hat and much worn canvas shoes brought jeers until he was "red in the face." But on his first at bat, Lajoie smashed a shot into the bleachers. The love affair was on. His reception by the fans during his eighty games with Fall River was equally as crazed as his 1903 celebration. According to one exuberant national sportswriter, Lajoie "had the descendants of Cotton Mather, Roger Williams, Miles Standish and kindred folk doing handsprings, turning cartwheels from sheer delight in the bleachers of Fall River and other towns in the league. For surely never before had such doings with the bludgeon been enacted on Pilgrim soil since the days of Lizzie Borden."

Lajoie was not to stay long at Fall River, however. His .429 batting average earned him a quickly issued ticket to the Philadelphia team in the new American League. Stardom was awaiting. When that call to the majors came, Lajoie was "full of running wild ambition." After picking up a few

hits with the Phillies, he immediately wrote to a friend in Woonsocket telling him that "…someday you're going to see the Lajoie name on top of the
batting list." It didn't take long.

As much as Fall River Fall River idolized him, the fact of the matter
was that Napoleon was born in Woonsocket, and the city of his birth never
wavered in its allegiance to him. Writing in 1911, a national reporter made
clear the crazed and sustained love affair between the city and its home-
grown prodigy: "Woonsocket never loses its mental balance but once a
year. That's when Larry goes back home. He always takes a run over to the
old town for summer holiday. It's also a holiday for everyone else in Woonsocket. They close the factories, blow the whistles, bring out the fire engine
and everything in their power to make fitting demonstration."

In November, 1900, Lajoie was honored by 50 citizens gathered in
Monument Hall in Woonsocket. He had by this time completed over four
full major league seasons, averaging .345 in the process. Called a player
"second to none," Lajoie was presented an inscribed gold headed ebony
cane by the grateful clan. The toastmaster seized the occasion to trumpet
civic pride proclaiming that Lajoie "has made the name of Woonsocket
heard all over the country and distinguished himself in his calling…base-
ball has now come to be an honorable profession." Even the zealous toast-
master did not good so far as to contend, as did one writer, that "the entire
state of Rhode Island would have slipped off into the Atlantic Ocean of
obscurity," if it were not for Lajoie. Kane made only vague allusion to the
earlier Flick-Lajoie confrontation that year in which the Emperor of Woonsocket's hand was fractured by a wall that had no respect for royalty. Of
course, if Kane had detailed every aspect of the fight, Lajoie would have
been that much more seen as being one of them.

The scores of Woonsocket folk who traveled to Boston to see Lajoie
when the Phillies came into town were loyal folk. In fact, even when their

Assuming a Napoleonic stance.

hero didn't play for the town team, the fans made clear their devotion. In a 1902 game in which Lajoie played for rival team Whitinsville against the Woonsocket Gyms, 8,000 fans rushed to Clinton Oval in Woonsocket. Over ten years later, in 1922, coming to Woonsocket and Mount St Charles as part of a barnstorming appearance, the *Woonsocket Wonder* again attracted a crowd of over 8,000 fans.

Lajoie accepted his cane with characteristic brevity and humility. "I'm not so good at giving speeches. I wished it were so that I might more strongly express my appreciation for the kindness you have shown. I thank you for your kind words, and I pledge that I will always conduct myself in a way that you will never be disappointed in me."

This bonding oath was a confirmation that honor could be had by the son of a shoemaker, son of a farmer, mine worker, mill worker. Almost forty years later, he would stand on a raised platform in Cooperstown with men of such common pedigree.

The unpretentious Lajoie understood the implications of the toast-master's words. It was not simply a matter of his success in batting and throwing the ball around. The youth of Woonsocket and all youth across the country could embrace not only the hero himself but the work ethic and exemplary character that could be their tickets to success, just as they had been for Lajoie. And the mill workers wiping sweat from their fore-heads, could claim him as being one of their own, as much a champion as any man. A rag to riches story, the young man who had played ball in the city's sandlots, had swept the floors of the Clinton cotton mill, had been a hack driver for lumber yards and funeral, and had spent short time with the fire department, was one of them.

Clearly, Napoleon Lajoie knew the Horatio Alger credo and be-lieved it worthy of retelling to youth. "There is luck to becoming a baseball player," he told boys across the country in an article for *American Boy*, "but the proportion of pluck is always greater… just as is the case for any fellow in any kind of work." Baseball was "work, and hard work, even if its play-ing in front of thousands." Not coincidentally, the title of one of Horatio Alger's books was *Pluck and Luck.*

Following Lajoie's extraordinary 1901 season, ubiquitous Toast-master Kane again had his moment to lay claim to their native son, who only six years earlier had played for *The Woonsockets* on a trotters track at Agricultural Field, now called Barry Field. Lajoie was in town as part of a barnstorming trip. As was the case in Fall River, workers took off early to see the 3:15 game. At one point, the game was interrupted so the love feast could be articulated. As he handed Napoleon a gold watch and chain, Kane proclaimed, "let this watch mean home to you and wherever you play or whatever city's name adorns your breast, we always want to know that Woonsocket is in your heart." According to newspaper accounts, Larry was visibly moved by the remarks. And perhaps he was energized. On the first pitch following, he clouted a drive into the Blackstone River, that ran by right field. A classic case of letting your bat do your talking.

Woonsocket, Rhode Island.

That evening in front of 120 citizens, Mayor Greene of Woonsocket called Lajoie "the greatest hero, the monarch of the diamond, the Napoleon of baseball." As if to affirm the Mayor's comparison, the next speaker told the story of an aghast history teacher who upon asking a student what was the greatest achievement of Napoleon was told, "Five hits for a total of 14 bases."

Throughout the night of adulation, Lajoie "kept his eyes upon the snowy linen to hide his embarrassment." Of course, he did have to turn his attention to the salad, "Salad a la Lajoie, Great." His thanks were quick and humble, as usual. He did address the 13-0 scrubbing the local team had suffered against his barnstormers. "They wanted to win and so did we. We won. If we did not, we would have left town and not been here tonight." Quintessential Lajoie.

Members of his family, two of his brothers, were at the dinner. Longtime residents of Woonsocket, they needed no direction as to how to get Monument Hall. They represented not only the Lajoie family, but the migration of French Canadians from Quebec to New England. From 1840 to 1930, 900,000 residents of Quebec province moved to New England seeking relieve from grinding poverty. The impoverished Lajoie family decided that they would take their 5 children and move from St Hyacinthe, Canada 20 miles outside of Montreal. After a brief two-year hiatus in Vermont, Jean Baptiste took his family to Woonsocket, where the mills offered more opportunity. Eager to employ French-Canadians since they were seen as good workers and non-unionized, these mills paid three times the wages offered in Canadian mills. Workers could earn $1.50 a day, as compared to the fifty-five cent a day wage in Canada.

Soon four of his children began work in those mills, working as cleaner in a cotton mill and spinners Counting Jean Baptiste's earning as a laborer and driver, the Lajoie family had five incomes to help them break even. On Sept 5, 1874, Napoleon Lajoie joined the clan. If a birth certificate scribbling is to be believed, he was the eighth of eleven children that were born to the Celina and Jean Baptiste. Eight years later, Jean Baptiste died of a heart attack while getting a hair cut in Woonsocket barbershop not that far from Monument Hall. He was 51. He left behind him a brood of eight, six sons and two daughters. Life would get that much more demanding. Young Napoleon would have to learn to make himself comfortable in various beds.

According to an 1885 Town Census, ten-year-old Napoleon Lajoie had a total school attendance of eleven months. He could read, but not write. At ten, he also fell in love with baseball. It was clear from the beginning that, however sweet his swing as a mill floor cleaner, the boy could swing the wagon tongue with the best of them. Lajoie recalls that teams that chose him were restricted to seven players to compensate for having the dark haired Sandy on their team.

If Lajoie could be assured that Woonsocket had a soft spot for their native son, Mr. Kane need not have worried that the young boy from Globe Village would not keep Woonsocket in his heart. In fact, during his pre-married years, Lajoie for the most part spent the off season in Woonsocket. One year he worked at a local pool room, spending cherished time with old buddies. Living with his widowed mom Celina, he enjoyed family life with his brothers and sisters. Woonsocket was the center of his affection. On one occasion, though, that loyalty was put to the test. During the seventh inning of a game in Boston, a fan who had come with a large contingent of Woonsocket followers, left his thirty cent seat, jumped over the railing, and ran to first baseman Lajoie. "Nap, old boy," he said, "I've got to get that eight o'clock back to little old Woonsocket. Stake me the two bucks, will you?" Unperturbed, Lajoie gave a high sign to the bench, and "his old neighbor" got his money. In addition to local allegiance, "Nap, old boy's" generosity might have been fueled by the good mood created by driving in seven of his team's nine runs by then.

For the rest of his life, Lajoie kept the cane given to him by the citizens of Woonsocket. It traveled from Woonsocket, to Cleveland and to his Florida homes. Upon his death, his niece knew that it should be given to the Cooperstown museum.

SOME FRENCH CONNECTIONS

Lajoie's French heritage no doubt contributed to his appeal and fed the romances concocted by the writers. On the cover of the *Stars of the National Game (1908)* Lajoie trods along dressed in Napoleonic garb. Of all the National and American teams represented on the cover, he is the

only recognizable figure (see page 53). He was literally the face of the franchise. The Cleveland fans had voted to name the team the Naps, of course, after their beloved superstar. Even when Nap resigned as the manager of the team, the fans again made clear they wanted to stay with the name. The point is that he was beloved beyond any convenience of his appearance or his name. It is hard then to argue with Grantland Rice's contention that never before was a player's name so identified with the team for which he played. No one in the hero worshipping era could claim such acknowledgement. Yes, Connie Mack and his straw hat sat upon the Athletics elephant, and yes, his players were called the Mackmen by scribes, but the team was not named after him. The Brooklyn team earlier had often been referred to as the Robins, after Wilbert Robinson their manager, but hardly was the association as profound and pictorial as Lajoie's. Robinson was not a player manager as was Lajoie. Indeed, his head might have fit on the body of the robin, but his portly body would have hardly fit, however much the robin's breast was puffed. Robinson was the better manager, however.

Napoleon Lajoie was born five years after the fall of Napoleon II, at a time when sympathies for the "luckless Emperor" were high. It was most likely he was named for the "little Napoleon." It was Napoleon the Big, Napoleon Bonaparte, who was worthy of direct comparison with the Emperor of the Diamond, however. Such Napoleonic comparisons carried some majesty and superiority and allowed for journalistic playfulness. Grantland Rice suggested that Napoleon Lajoie helped restore Napoleon Bonaparte's fading renown. In 1915, a poem in *Base Ball Magazine* accomplished such fan education. The reader learns of Napoleon's war tactics: "He walloped foes right on the nose and smote them hip and thigh." The poem also addresses his opening marital strategy saying that he used a disabling frontal attack followed by a two punch knock out, twin blows delivered to the opponent's torso. None of this military acumen, however, made him the equal of Napoleon Lajoie: "Yes, Boney earned some renown but he never swung a wagon tongue and copped a baseball game while all the crowd were howling loud. He never dug his cleats and with his ash poled a smash against the bleacher seats."

According to the poem, baseball 's "Slamming King of Swat corralled the piping hot ball and swung a mace with kingly grace." And so, although in battle Napoleon was something else," it was time to share his throne for "when chaps compare these Naps, each peerless in his way, of course each man who is a fan will pull for Lajoie (La ZHO way)."

A popular song was unwilling to be so gracious to the French Emperor:

Who lost out in the battle of Waterloo?
I don't know. I don't know.
They say 'twas Na-po-le-on
Maybe it's true
Maybe so. I don't know
The pink sheets don't print no stories about him today
'Cause he could never hold down that old second base
    Like his namesake- La-zho-way.

Of course, with his French heritage came ethnic slurs. He was frequently called "the Big Frog." Lajoie took no offense. He had himself often used ethnic slurs in provoking his opponents. No doubt he took some pride in being called *the French Devil* by future Hall of Fame manager and player Clark Griffith. His French heritage was reason for his rejection by Giant owner Freedman who refused to sign him telling his scout, "No Frenchman or Dutch. Get me Irish."

Lajoie took no offense in the good natured ribbing of English spoken French style. Accordingly, he enjoyed hearing the story told by one of his friends about a French-Canadian who decided to see Lajoie play in Fall River:

Wan day I have some monee on ma clo's, and I think it bout time I make some small veezet on Fall River and see ma fren 'Poleon play. So I buy me a tiquet and go to Fall Reveer. I got me der early an 'tak wan seet jus'back de catcher mon. Begosh, I neverair see such beeg criowd as dere was Dat day. It makes me proud to see da way ma fren 'Poleon peek up de ball no maittaire how hard she get hit.

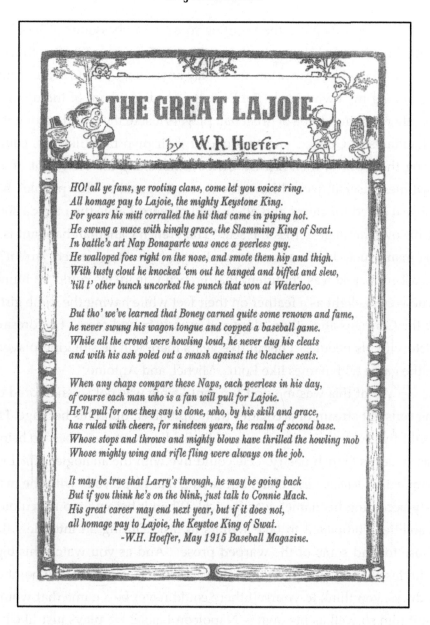

THE GREAT LAJOIE
by W.R. Hoefer.

HO! all ye fans, ye rooting clans, come let you voices ring.
All homage pay to Lajoie, the mighty Keystone King.
For years his mitt corralled the hit that came in piping hot.
He swung a mace with kingly grace, the Slamming King of Swat.
In battle's art Nap Bonaparte was once a peerless guy.
He walloped foes right on the nose, and smote them hip and thigh.
With lusty clout he knocked 'em out he banged and biffed and slew,
'till t' other bunch uncorked the punch that won at Waterloo.

But tho' we've learned that Boney carned quite some renown and fame,
he never swung his wagon tongue and copped a baseball game.
While all the crowd were howling loud, he never dug his cleats
and with his ash poled out a smash against the bleacher seats.

When any chaps compare these Naps, each peerless in his day,
of course each man who is a fan will pull for Lajoie.
He'll pull for one they say is done, who, by his skill and grace,
has ruled with cheers, for nineteen years, the realm of second base.
Whose stops and throws and mighty blows have thrilled the howling mob
Whose mighty wing and rifle fling were always on the job.

It may be true that Larry's through, he may be going back
But if you think he's on the blink, just talk to Connie Mack.
His great career may end next year, but if it does not,
all homage pay to Lajoie, the Keystoe King of Swat.
                                    -W.H. Hoeffer, May 1915 Baseball Magazine.

Joining in the fun, Lajoie told the friend that upon signing with Fall River he had told the owner that "By gar, she's a good monee."

Lajoie was more than willing to be an ambassador of baseball spreading the word among his fellow French Canadians." I often think," he said "that when I grow too old to play anymore, I will do some scouting among my own people-the French Canadians. I am of the opinion that there are hundreds of great ball players lost to the world among the inhabitants of Quebec, and that one of their own race, like me, could bring them out of their shells." After establishing his view that of all pastimes baseball would have the greatest appeal to "his people" because it asked for clever and all-around players, Lajoie then took a shot at his own heritage across the sea. "The French Canadian habitant is a big man. Queer how our cousins in France have degenerated, isn't it?" he asked. Lajoie was confident that French-Canadians could be found who were as light as a feather on their feet while having the same girth as the Germans and other "slow and muscle bound races" He foresaw victory to his people. "I bet in five years there will be slugging players in the game with names like Louis, Michel, and Antoine."

All of this was in good fun, but Lajoie was not so enamored of the constant stream of accolades that capitalized upon his heritage. He could live with the inane similes. His fielding was described as being "as sweet as French pastry." He could live with the analogies. *The Emperor of the Diamond was* okay, but saying that he played "with the majesty becoming his name" was farcical. When it became too ridiculous, Lajoie felt compelled to take writers to task. During an interview, he chose to read some of the warped prose: "And as you watch this big, grim fascinating Frenchman, solemn and serious almost to the point of sadness, you think to yourself there could never be a name that would befit him so well as his own -- Napoleon Lajoie. He plays just like his name sounds. His every movement harmonizes with the deep stately poetry of that name." Lajoie put the paper down. "I wish my dad would have read that. O Me, O My."

Lajoie found another article to ridicule. "Listen to this -- an eye filling d'Artagnan whose every pose was a picture- a handsome fellow, big and dark, with bold features, he wears his cap cocked on the side of his head, which is covered with thick, dark, wavy hair. And the Big Frenchman wears the uniform roll collar of the day casually turned up to make an attractive frame for his face." Lajoie rolled his eyes and continued the litany of the love fest: Long, clean cut mouth…. big finely chiseled nose with a dimple on his chin… a pair of round soft eyes that seem to look right into you and yet are soft, tender, and gentle."

Lajoie looked up. "Soft and tender and gentle? Aren't I the original come on?" He laughed, "How do I keep my marriage together after my wife reads all this?"

"An eye-filling d'Artagnan… he wears his cap cocked on the side of his head, which is covered with thick, dark, wavy hair."

However uncomfortable Lajoie was with the consequences real and imagined of the adulation showered upon him, he knew that America's love affair with baseball was a good thing for him and for the game. Spinning turnstiles and rabid fans, even the overly zealous ones, translated into dollar signs for him and many others. There is no doubt that Napoleon Lajoie's appearance contributed to his popularity. He was handsome, powerfully man, standing six foot one and weighing about 195. A writer commented that it was possible to hear the ladies sighing as they watched him play, "their soft purring pencils" composing love letters. In point of fact, Napoleon received so many of such letters that he had to create a mimeographed response sheet that acknowledged their interest without encouraging any amorous follow up.

Lajoie was featured as the sole player in a Parker Brothers baseball card game.

Lajoie's sex appeal must have been a contributing factor in his selection to appear in the Coke ad. In reality, Coke executives had little choice. Diminuative Eddie Collins wasn't exactly pulp material. Knobby kneed Wagner? No. And Cobb coming towards them might cause the family to scatter in fear. As in many things, Lajoie saw no reason not to capitalize on what was given. However, he had the character and sense to repeatedly turndown offers to appear in dime shows showing off his physique. No reason to think that Mrs. Lajoie would have been so understanding in this case.

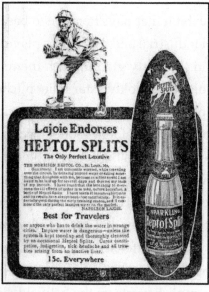

Tobacco, sports equipment companies and others relentlessly sought Lajoie's endorsements.

AND THEN THERE WAS CLEVELAND, OF COURSE

Traveling to Woonsocket today, visitors come in good numbers to visit a proud jewel of the city -- the Museum of Work and Culture. On the first floor of the museum is a wonderful recreation of life in the mills. The life of four Lajoie boys went through these mills, including for a brief time, Napoleon Lajoie. On the second floor of the museum is an exhibit that pays homage to baseball in the Blackstone Valley. Town and industrial and mill teams players standing proudly with their mates amid the dusty gloom. With them, Hall of Famers Gabby Harnett and Lajoie and Brooklyn star relief pitcher Clem Labine. In the corner of one display is a wooden horseshoe with a baseball bat. It was carved by Woonsocket resident Lionel Lajoie, Napoleon's nephew, to commemorate Cleveland's honoring of their hero, his uncle, upon for his ten year of service to Forest City. The actual horseshoe was nine feet tall, but Lionel had a life. The highlight of Lajoie Day, the horseshoe was festooned with 1,009 silver dollars contributions from the fans.

The letter sent out to fans by the Cleveland News soliciting these contributions, made clear that the homage was not only "Our Larry's" accomplishments on the ballfield. For one thing, it was also based upon understanding that he has rescued a floundering baseball town:

In honor of the player who has done more to baseball on its high plane in Cleveland than any other individual, we want 1,000 or more of our fans to show their appreciation of the work of Napoleon Lajoie as a member of the Naps day in and day out for ten years by purpose of purchasing an immense thousand-dollar horseshoe, the same to be presented to the man who has brought everlasting fame to Cleveland as a baseball town.

Fans knew full well that Cleveland baseball was teetering on the ledge. The Bronchos were not exactly the talk of the town. The Lajoie rocket sent by Connie Mack in 1902 was on a rescue mission. Not only to keep the American League afloat but to bring welcomed rain to the parched Cleveland baseball scene. The newspaper spoke on behalf of all the many thankful cranks rescued from disillusionment with the game and on behalf of those on all levels who lined their pockets. It must have been a Lebron James-like resurrection for Cleveland over a hundred years earlier.

Lajoie called the Cleveland fans' recognition of him for ten years of service the most memorable day of his career. The fans themselves contributed the 1,009 silver dollars in the horseshoe.

In 1908, four years before the paper's appeal, a prominent Cleveland journalist wrote about Lajoie as part of a series of stories on Cleveland's most esteemed citizens. Again the theme was pride in Lajoie. The people of Cleveland, "unfailingly tipped their hat to him as a player and person." Lajoie was said to be "a household word, written about as much as President Taft." And so often had Lajoie been photographed that "his features are familiar to every street gamin and to every millionaire clubman." The article lays the foundation for that popularity, claiming that Lajoie hadn't had his head turned by fame. He was the same Larry as he was when he was discovered, still carrying "the bashfulness and modesty of a schoolboy."

The newspaper solicitation for silver dollars plagiarized the "household" wording of the above article, even as it made clear that there was another reason that Lajoie was appreciated. That reason too had a moral tinge to it.

Napoleon Lajoie… it is a name that has been a household word in Cleveland since 1902… Here is a player who is regarded as one of the brightest lights of the game, this or any other age. There isn't a man, woman, or child but will say that Larry has always given the fans the very best that is in him.

This was the rest of the story then. Larry had proven his character and commitment. He had given his best, honored the contract between a baseball star and its fans. If Nap's professed purpose in life was "to look every man in the eye," the citizens of Cleveland confirmed he had delivered on the goods. No different than the fan adulation of Peter Reiser of the Dodgers in the 1950's, or Trot Nixon or Dustin Pedroia of the Red Sox's, honesty of effort has always been appreciated. In some towns. It is a necessary although not always sufficient ingredient of fan acceptance.

Throw in superior performance on the field and your stock raises. Throw in exemplary character off the field, and you make Standard and Poor's

Lajoie Day was a grand day, full of music and tributes, but the malcontent in the crowd might have been thinking that in those ten years Larry had not delivered a pennant to the people of Cleveland. He never was to do so. If the horseshoe was intended to not only honor Larry but bring him and Cleveland luck, it failed. Perhaps that could be attributed to the dastardly behavior of the Boston players, who, as was tradition, walked backwards through the horseshoe taking away its power in the process.

Nevertheless, Lajoie was moved by the tribute, so much so that he called it the greatest moment in his career. He was always quick to remind everyone that a dollar was a lot of money in those days. Throughout his retirement, Nap repeatedly said that his failure to win a pennant for Cleveland was his greatest regret. "One chance to compete in a World Series, even if I did not draw one cent for my services-and I could go into retirement feeling I had enjoyed all the good things which can be had from baseball." Surprisingly, no one ever asked him if he would trade the horseshoe for a pennant. Perhaps they were too civil. Nonetheless, the answer would have been, "Hell, yes."

AND THEN THERE WAS THE COUNTRY

As they say today, the Lajoie fan base "traveled well," but his great popularity went well beyond the three cities that claimed him- Woonsocket, Fall River, and Cleveland. A Boston scribe acknowledged that every city has its "favorite son but there is only one Lajoie" and every baseball city in the country paid him tribute. As if to affirm the point, *The Boston Globe* asserted that "Lajoie pleased the gallery more than the great Wagner."

*It was said of Lajoie that even half interested fans
would flock to their home park to see him play.*

The same writer translated the dollar sense of that adoration. "He has no equal. In less than two weeks, Lajoie earned one half of his salary. Five thousand of the six thousand fans who attended today's game at the Huntington Grounds were due to Lajoie." Having gone to the trouble to tabulate Lajoie's yearly salary at $28 per hour, the writer concluded that he was a bargain. In Detroit, Cobb's world, Lajoie also drew well. On Lajoie's first game in Detroit, he was greeted by thousands of French speaking fans, including a good size French-Canadian contingent, all eager to see "le plus fame aux jouer de base-ball qui soit passe aux Etats-Unis depuis un grand nombre d'annees." That trip must have been slightly deflating for when they addressed him in French, the sheepish Lajoie had no response to speak of (excuse the pun); he had lost any fluency in French by the age of seven.

Lajoie's extraordinary performances in the first years of the American League existence not only gave the league vital footing but also brought nationwide superstar recognition. "We had no great draw outside of Lajoie," contended one of the league owners." He was the idol of the circuit," added another American League executive. In 1904, a *Boston Globe* sportswriter agreed saying that although every city has its favorite son, "...there is only one Lajoie, and every baseball city in the country pays tribute to him. He is the king of them all." Indeed, Lajoie was often referred to as *King Larry*. Such regal recognition fit seamlessly with the New York Press' view of Lajoie, written in 1906, "...Of all the thousands of cracking good men who have won laurels on the diamond since baseball became the national game, it is the unanimous opinion that none ever equaled Larry...." The words were a tribute to Lajoie's character, as well as his talent. Famous sportswriter Frederic Lieb in 1911 contended that thousands of "half-fans" only visited their home ball park" if King Larry was the stellar attraction." He had to be seen. Having seen Cobb, Wagner, and other stars of the game, Hall of Fame Umpire Evans in 1919 proclaimed, "I seriously doubt if any player in the history of the game was more universally popular." Of course, the Sultan of Swat had barely arrived on the scene by this time.

Perhaps the best and most impressive confirmation of Lajoie's national drawing power came from Charles Hughes, one of the founders of Baseball Writers Association. "I don't think that either Cobb or Wagner drew in any extra customers to speak of, "said Hughes, with amazement. "Charlie Comiskey, the old Roman owner of the White Sox, told me one day that Lajoie stood alone in fan gate attraction."

Cy Young spoke of another allegiance. "Larry was such an idol that crowds followed him down the street...kids worshipped him, and I have been told that when he endorsed a certain brand of tobacco, half the kids in the nation got sick giving the foul weed a tryout in the hope that it would make them sluggers like Lajoie.... the children followed him around like the Pied Piper." Enough said.

The idea being to pin the tail on the bat,
Lajoie is featured in this birthday party game for kids.

CHAPTER THIRTEEN

Unforgotten Roots

Wearing a dark suit and a black derby hat, the tall man walked up to the feisty manager of the NY Giants. "Mr. McGraw, my name is Charles Victory Faust. I live over in Kansas, and a few weeks ago I went to a fortune teller who told me that if I joined the NY Giants and pitch for them that they would win the pennant. "

McGraw tossed him a glove. "I'll get a catcher's mitt and we'll see what you've got." Before pitching, Faust gave McGraw his signals, didn't want to hurt him. McGraw gave him one of those signals and Faust's windup began, a windup like a windmill, both arms going around in circles for quite a while before the pitch was released. Regardless of the signal given, there was no difference in the pitches. All had barely enough speed to break a pane of glass.

After a few minutes of catching Faust barehanded, McGraw decided it was time for some fun. He invited Faust to show him his hitting and running skills. On the first pitch, Faust dribbled one to the shortstop who deliberately juggled the ball as Faust circled first and slid into second. As the shortstop continued his charade of having difficulty corralling the ball, Faust proceeded to third and finally to home, sliding dramatically into each base. All of this without taking off his suit.

That night, the superstitious McGraw announced, "We're taking Charlie along to help us win the pennant." McGraw paid for all of Charlie's traveling costs, including his daily haircut and massage and tips for waiters. The Giants won the pennant that year, 1911. The next year, Faust again appeared in training camp, again warmed up during every game, and again the Giants won the pennant. 1913 was Faust's breakout year. Not only did he yet again lead the Giants to a pennant, but since by this time he was fan favorite and a drawing card, McGraw finally gave him his big chance to pitch in the majors. In an already decided game. Faust's nothing ball pitches baffled Cincinnati, and he pitched a full scoreless inning.

Despite his lifetime 0.00 ERA, Charles Victory Faust never got a Giant contract. During that season, however, Charles got a contract on Broadway, mimicking the greats of the game - Cobb, Mathewson, Wagner - in a short comedic sketch. He was gone four days to fulfill his thespian responsibilities. The Giants lost all four games.

Not many players were as superstitious as John McGraw. He made his Giants don black broadcloth uniforms in the World Series against Connie Mack's A's. Perhaps he should have made the players hold black cats as well for the Giants again lost a World Series to the Mackmen. Even Charles Victory Faust was rendered impotent. He was a Payton Manning racking up regular season victories but faltering in the post season.

"I live over in Kansas. I went to a fortuneteller who told me that if I joined the New York Giants and pitched for them, they would win the pennant." – Charles Faust

The fact is that the game touted as a game of science never kicked superstition out of bed, far from it. In effect, Charles Faust was a team mascot. As such, he was part of baseball's superstition traditions. Mascots were the human rabbit's foot. It didn't matter if they were cute and cherubic. Or ugly and devilish. They could come to the field drunk. No requirement for demeanor. They were the insurance policy that voodoo wouldn't step on the field. When it did, they were let go. In the meantime, they traveled with the team, ate at the hotels, were paid something. Such small expenses were sound investment leverage against bad luck. Mascots found their ways into team photos and donned the uniforms of their employers. They were not dressed intended to delighted young fans, nor did they take on their opposing mascot in field competitions. Theirs was serious work.

The mascots of the Athletics and Yankees: human rabbit's feet.

Everyone had a mascot. Connie Mack's mascot during the 1915 season was a behemoth easily over 300 pounds. His uniform buttons threatening to burst when he leaned over, he was barely able to field a ground ball. In contrast, the Yankees that same year had a waif of a child, a sprite. His uniform hung from him and even the small glove of the times dwarfed his small hand and covered his impish face.

The 1909 Tigers had found their mascot the year before, a homeless boy of eleven trying to find shelter in the nooks and crannies of Bennett Field. His name was Ulysses Harrison, but the Tigers called him 'Lil' Rastus. Did that boy play or even like baseball? Didn't matter. The next year, when the Tigers reeled off a long winning streak, he became Ty Cobb's special good luck charm. Man of science, man of profound bigotry, Cobb, nevertheless, wanted every advantage. Described by one paper as "the Ethiopian's main defender and patron," the youth was snuck aboard trains, lodged in the clubhouse and slipped into whites-only hotels on the road trips. Following the 1909 regular season, the Tigers went on to lose their third consecutive World Series and a toothless Cobb batted but .231. Like Victory Faust, Harrison was unable to break a Series jinx, and was forced into early retirement. For mascots, it was all about "what have you done for me lately?" Ulysses, however, was brought home to Georgia and made a domestic servant. Over the years the two remained friends, as much as that term could accommodate the patronizing and belittling bigotry of Cobb.

Napoleon Lajoie decision to also make a homeless boy the team's mascot, this one using League Park as a warming plate, had no strings attached. Of course, it didn't hurt that the nine-year- old boy loved baseball and was pretty good at it. Did Petie Powers bring the Cleveland team or Lajoie good luck? Not really, but superstition had no part of his inclusion into the Naps' family.

An orphan boy, a "street Arab," Petie Powers spent his day selling newspapers and his night shooting craps. Many nights he slept on the streets. He also spent his time loitering around League Park, trying to slip in unseen to see his heroes or at the very least gain a glimpse of them as they entered or left the park. Fortunately for him, one player took special notice.

The photo from the 1902 Boston Globe shows Napoleon Lajoie standing next to Petie. Petie is the one in the knickers. The relationship between the two is described in the attending article as "part of the Romance of the Baseball Diamond." That is to say" the Great Lajoie" had taken the boy under his wings and was teaching him America's Game. Lajoie never legally adopted the boy, but he made him the Cleveland Naps mascot for two years. According to the paper, Lajoie "saw to it that the boy was well-dressed and properly looked after" while the team was on the road, unlike Cobb's rabbit foot who had to be kept in the team's pocket at all times. Lajoie also paid for Pettie's education. As much as he would certainly have wanted to skip the classroom life, Pettie was required to meet obligations, and so he joined the team after school let out.

THE STORY OF "PETIE"

A Few Weeks Ago a Street Arab in Cleveland— Now an Aspirant to the Shoes of the Great Lajoie

Lajoie saw to it that "the smart little fellow" was educated and taught the skills of the game. Did Lajoie see himself in the young boy?

Petie was grateful to his benefactor. "He's just like my father. I love him." And when Lajoie took ill during a part of the 1903 season, Pettie was there to help as best he could. The boy educated in the streets was smart enough to know a good thing when he saw it. "I'm going to nurse it to the limit," he proclaimed, "Why not? Three square meals a day, best hotels, traveling in police cars, sitting on the bench." Eager to become the "real thing in baseball," he also willingly subjected himself to Lajoie's tutelage in developing his baseball skills. Like many a young boy dreaming that stardom awaited, he dreamed big, already time-lining his eventual replacement of Lajoie on the national baseball scene. "He's (Lajoie) in a class by himself," Petie reasoned, "but when I get old enough, he will be out of the game, and I will fill his shoes in great style." Almost sounds as if Lajoie was lucky that he wasn't seen as a roadblock to the future plans of the ambitious upstart. What a story it would have been for that baseball romance if Pettie had filled his benefactor's shoes. In fact, Petie later did play semi-professional ball for a team in Ohio and was described as "a cooking good player."

Lajoie never spoke much about Petie, only saying that Petie was "a smart little fellow but neglected." It is a curious photo, begging the question why a man who was comfortable with his own humble roots would dress the adopted lad in such a silver spoon outfit- riding crop and all- and while apparelling himself in a rather dandified outfit. The photo's cutline offers little insight. "Petie and Lajoie" is not exactly revelatory. There may have been humorous intent on a few levels. Easier to interpret would have been a bat in Petie's hand and a ball in Lajoie's.

It's hardly a stretch to think though that Lajoie saw in Petie a boy who reminded him of himself. Lajoie had lost his father when he was five, leaving behind a wife and eight children. Although not an orphan, he moved about frequently, as the family struggled to provide him and themselves a place to live. Over the course of six years, he is listed as living at nine different addresses. His formal education ended by the time he was eight and his obsession with playing baseball and its heroes began around ten years of age. At night, he dreamed that someday he would be the next Cap Anson, one of the greatest players of the time. By day, he took to the street to play ball and prove his worth. Those street were busy and dangerous. The commercial world filled them with wagon carts and trolleys, merciless agents of capitalism that had no regard for the silliness of seriously played games.

Mrs. Lajoie understood that danger lurked behind the joyful cries of the kids playing ball. Her frightened and demanding calls to her son to return home rang in his ears. The ten year-old, however, was not beyond resorting to deception to silence these calls. Ever so clever lads, Napoleon and his fellow street urchins concocted a plan, agreeing that his new name would be "Sandy," hardly a red flag that would alert a vigilant mother that her swarthy child was playing in the streets outside. And so, as Nap's mates chased Sandy's line drive ricocheting off the façade of the meat market storefront and heading towards the fast approaching horse-drawn delivery wagon, a blissfully ignorant Mrs. Lajoie turned her attention to the family's economic realities. At five cents a pound, sugar was on the rise. Eggs were now twelve cents a dozen. She knew how to make due though. Losing Philippe two years ago had been so hard, but she would make due. No choice but to make hard choices that saddened her. The children's money helped though. She knew the noise of the mill machines was deafening. They always came home complaining their ears rang. She knew why the girls wore black. They always needed a bath. She didn't know how many times children were used to raise a lever or grab a bob, or clear an obstruction as the merciless machines raged but a few inches from their small fingers. She didn't know that once a diligent fellow employee swept her son Napoleon's hand away just before it was to be ensnared by the machine that had been fed human flesh before.

No doubt Lajoie understood the struggles of children caught in the crosshairs of economic crisis. His concern for them went beyond helping Petie Powers. A frequent visitor and correspondent was the director of the Jewish Asylum for the Homeless. Larry's efforts were enthusiastically supported and expanded by his wife, Myrtle. They married in 1902. Pettie's mascot tenure began around the same time. Lajoie mentioned that it had taken him weeks to get the courage to seek an introduction to the woman whose applause at the ball park meant something special. The couple was never to have children, but their interest in helping less fortunate kids was sincere and sustained.

Mrs. Lajoie appreciated her new esteem. "It is better to be Mrs. Lajoie than Mrs. Taft. It's better to be the wife of the best ball player in the world, and that's what they say Larry is." She capitalized upon that fame to help the Petie Powers children of the world. One Cleveland paper made clear that one of the reasons the Lajoies were "held in great affection by their home city" was their acts of humanity in reaching out to the city's children. Mrs. Lajoie seemed especially devoted to helping them. Her commitment to the children was authentic and sustained: "Mrs. Lajoie was always figuring on a way to give fun to the kids," said the paper. Each year, she sponsored a special event for orphaned children. One year, soliciting the help of the Cleveland Automobile Club, she arranged a joyful parade of cars that carried 2,300 youngsters through the streets of Cleveland. The tour stopped for picnics in the city's parks and culminated in an outing at the city's beaches and amusement parks. Speaking of the twenty-four kids packed in Mrs. Lajoie's car, the paper proclaimed that the children's "gay laughter and happy chatter caused everyone they passed to wear a smile."

CHAPTER FOURTEEN

"*You Will, Will You?*"

Connie Mack and the owners of the newly minted American League needed a few talented and popular cornerstone players. Delighted that such a mighty star as Lajoie would consider changing leagues, Mack tried to induced Lajoie to abandon his contract with the National League's Philadelphia Phillies to join Connie's cross-town rivals, the Athletics. Mack offered Lajoie a substantial raise, from $2,400 to $4,000 a year, that $2,400 being the highest salary the National League permitted. Of course, the $1,600 raise was an attractive and fair reward for his .346 batting average in 1900. But there was more to La-joie's decision to jump into Connie's arm. Lajoie felt that in the previous year Phillies owner Colonel John I. Rogers had earlier tried to pull a fast one on him. Both coming off marvelous seasons, teammates Ed De-lahanty and Napoleon Lajoie, had secretly agreed to hold out, demand-ing more than the $2,400 maximum. Rogers seemingly gave in, offering Lajoie $2,600 while telling him that was the same amount he was giving to Delehanty. In reality, Delehanty was given $3,000. Rogers' deception outraged Lajoie. He did not begrudge Delehanty the extra money, the two were friends and roommates. It was the inequity and deceit that fueled his resolve to leave ship. Years later, Lajoie made clear his expec-tation of the owner, saying that all he had asked of Rogers was that, "he would tell me the truth about salaries paid to other members of the team." No doubt, the satisfaction of getting a $1,600 raise soothed his moral outrage at being lied to and duped out of $400.

In reality, Rogers had a few strikes against him. For one thing, he stood for the type of man Lajoie couldn't stomach- a duplicitous man in love with himself, a power broking user of others. Lajoie later re-counted the nature of Colonel Rogers saying that Rogers was, "…a man fond of arguing… who loved writing interminable letters to newspapers about the fine points of baseball law." His ego was a prickling point for Lajoie. According to Lajoie, Rogers "considered himself a parliamentar-ian without peer." Lajoie never liked know-it-all's, be they fans, other players, or owners. Strike one.

In a conversation with a friend, Lajoie told him that his goal in life was "to be able to live a life so that I could look everybody in the eye." Now in his sixties, he related how Rogers had violated such a moral imperative. With simmering indignation, he recalled Rogers bar-gaining style:

The average player seeking but a $100 raise had no chance with Rogers. 'What's that you say? One hundred dollars? Where would my wife and children obtain food if I were to raise you that amount?' Rogers would then assume such a crestfallen appearance that the player would slink out of his office ashamed of himself.

There was to Lajoie great injustice in such pretense. Today, such melodramatic bargaining would be dismissed, if not laughed at. Rogers evidently depended on the player to show respect, believe what was said, and make himself the miscreant. That this charade could be delivered on an intimate eye-to-eye level made it that much more reprehensible. Strike two.

Time for strike three. When both teams played in Philadelphia the year of Lajoie's jump to the Athletics, Lajoie's Athletics outdrew their National League counterpart by 10,000 fans. Incensed, Rogers went to court to determine the validity of the reserve clause. A lower Pennsylvania court ruled it illegal. Outraged, Rogers declared that the cases had hardly been tried in a judicious manner, that the judge had objected to sitting in hot weather and so his decisions were arbitrary and bias. Pontificating that not to reverse the decision would be to permit "the miscarriage of justice through tricks and quibbles," Rogers went to the State Supreme Court. Within a year, the injunction was reversed and a permanent injunction forbidding Lajoie from playing in Philadelphia was issued. Traveling on the train, crossing into the city limits of Philadelphia, Lajoie was transformed from a law abiding man to a fugitive from justice. However, since New York and Missouri courts upheld the illegality of the reserve clause, it was in Philadelphia alone that Lajoie was an outlaw. Lajoie was later to contend that if the National League had won the courtroom battle outside of Philadelphia, the American

League would have collapsed; a distinct possibility. Ever vigilant in protecting his earnings against the possible demise of the league, the always circumspect Lajoie had insisted that Mack deposit his $4,000 in a bank; a friend made the withdrawals. Reviewing Lajoie's astonishing performance for his fledgling American League, Mack must have considered that $4,000 the shrewdest investment he had ever made.

Ever resourceful, Mack the next season traded Lajoie to Cleveland; the league was not going to lose the jewel in their crown of credibility. The trade did not, however, change things; Lajoie was still a wanted man, and Philadelphia's men in blue took their manhunt seriously. As soon as the rail coach carrying the Cleveland team pulled into the city of Brotherly Love, they boarded the train, searching everywhere in the station. They inevitably charged into the Cleveland team's coach, demanding to know the whereabouts of the scalawag. With great feigned dismay, Manager Armour expressed his despair at the fruitless search. "I've looked high and low," he sighed," but he's not here." As the officers mumbled obsscenities, he stoked the fires of mockery. "If he ain't in the front trying to get some idea on how to run a choo-choo from the driver," Armour continued, "I guess he's taken French leave again. That's Frenchie's worst habit. He's jumped your club as well, hasn't he?"

The fuming officers headed to the hotel to continue their search.

The ruse was repeated each time the police interrogated the players, never failing to bring laughter from them and profanity from the frustrated pursuers. In reality, "Frenchie" had detoured to Atlantic City and professed enjoying the paid vacation. But to begin that vacation he had to often jump the passenger train transporting the Naps and hop onto the freight rails. Arriving in Atlantic City disheveled and dirty, cinders in his hair and black smudges on his face. Lajoie put everything in perspective. "When I was a boy in Rhode Island and talked about being a ballplayer, my dad would say: 'I'd hate to see my boy become a tramp.' After long rides on freight trains, I'm afraid that I looked the part of a hobo."

The pressures of the injunction drove some players back to Rogers, including Elmer Frick and Chick Fraser. Lajoie also returned to Philadelphia, but only to use the Phillies field to practice when they were on the road. Nevertheless, finally wearied by the stress, Lajoie was ready to return to the National League and the Phillies. Flush with victory, the owner of the Phillies John Rogers decided to extract his pound of flesh and assert his dominion. During a face-to-face with Lajoie, he made it clear that Lajoie was going to be fined several hundred dollars for jumping. Strike three.

"You will, will you?" thundered Lajoie. "Not if I can get a job selling scorecards." He stormed out of the office and back into the arms of the American League. End of case. The beneficiary of Rogers' misguided power play, Mack promptly sent Lajoie to Cleveland, who as mentioned, played without Lajoie when they were in Philly.

Normally affable Napoleon Lajoie was not to be used. The sense that no one could exercise their will against him was strong. When he identified the right of a situation, it was especially dangerous to back him into a corner or go high-hat on him. One wonders if he would have been able to take orders in the mills of Woonsocket or in the fire department hierarchy. However, Lajoie himself always had an open heart for those who came to him for financial help, many of whom would conveniently claim to be ex-ballplayers. Although no doubt Lajoie saw through the story of their professed baseball roots story, he saw their real need. Invariably, he'd sent them off with a few bucks and a quick piece of advice about the virtues of hard work and "stick-to-it-if-ness." No self-righteous lectures and most assuredly, no Rogerian guilt trip about how Mrs. Lajoie and he were on a shoestring and might lose the farm if he acquiesced to the request. He did have a Puritan work ethic, however. Fellow employ-ees at the tire store at which Lajoie worked after all baseball positions had ended marveled that when things got slow at work, he would leave his desk, pick up the broom and sweep the floors. Maybe such were recidi-vist behaviors from his floor sweeping days at the mills in Woonsocket.

Despite his dislike of Rogers, despite his testing of the reserve clause, Lajoie was not a rebel or malcontent. A contract went both

Connie opened the door to the newly-minted American League and Lajoie walked right in.

ways, and he had an obligation to perform. He needed to live up to the faith owners and fans put in him to do so. Asked by one of his closest friends what was his greatest ambition, Lajoie replied "to win a pennant for the Cleveland club. Not that I seek the glory but that I think it the best way to show my employers my appreciation for what they do for me." He had shown his allegiance to men who had met their side of the bargain. In 1902, John McGraw came a courtin'. The signing of Lajoie would be a death wound to the American League. McGraw offered Lajoie the highest salary ever offered a player- $25,000 for two years. Under contract with Cleveland, for $25,000 for three years, Lajoie nevertheless refused to entertain the offer. "Not for me, I've signed with Cleveland and all the money in the world will not tempt me to break that contract." Morality 101.

In his letter of resignation from his managerial position six years later, Lajoie confirmed his feeling that a contract also carried the moral imperative of meeting your end of the bargain. In his letter to the fans, he expressed the hope that someone else could do more justice to the fans who rightfully expect and deserve more. As stated, they knew such proclamation was not a grandstanding. When again asked to decide what name the team should now be given with Lajoie on the managerial sidelines, they voted to keep the team's name-the Naps.

This is not to say that Lajoie embraced all those fans. He did not believe that since fans paid for tickets or bought newspapers, they were entitled to say what they wanted. Often he defended in the press his players from rumors and fan accusations about their character and commitment.

There are many stories about players who went into the stands to confront catcalling blowhearts and cowards who launched their attacks within what they thought was the safety of the stands. In Lajoie's case, such fans were safe, but it was a matter of venue. Speaking about those fans that abuse and misrepresent players, Lajoie mentioned one on the street who within earshot had proclaimed that "Larry was rotten today. Saw the big boob sousing with his bunch of fellows." In reality, "Larry" had spent a quiet evening with friends. According to Lajoie, that fan "ended against a telegraph pole."

And what about those fans who one night came after manager Lajoie, attacking as foolhardy his use of pitchers or of the hit and run? What if they confronted him face to face? Such a fan, said Lajoie, "would be lucky to escape with his life."

Lajoie had confrontations with the Cleveland managers that followed him, just as players did with him during his tenure as manager. Most had to do with being dropped in the lineup or not getting opportunities to prove himself. He was sensitive also about being told how to play the game. He went public with his ire aimed at one of the managers who had replaced him with the Naps -- Joe Birmingham. For one thing Birmingham, then 28, had the nerve to bench a slumping Lajoie. But more importantly, if Nap was reluctant to tell others how to hit, he was sure as hell not going to take instruction from a no-name years his junior. Birmingham was in primary school when Lajoie was hitting .300 contended Lajoie. That a such a "bush league" career .250 hitter felt he had alicense to lecture was preposterous. That "Birmingham couldn't tell a man what to do without speaking to him as if he were a dog" brought things to a boil. No one would speak to Lajoie as if he were a subordinate.

Lajoie put up with the effrontery because "it's worth a good wad of cash to sit on the same bench with such a man." Money and security then won out even as anger simmered. In this case, pragmatism put a sleeper hold on his moral indignation. Lajoie's assessment of Birmingham's managerial effectiveness seemed on target. The next season would be a disaster, as the Naps lost 102 games, and in 1915, he was fired after only 28 games.

Without a doubt, Lajoie the manager would not have put up with a player going public with his gripes to the press as Lajoie the player did. We can assume he had first gone to Birmingham, following the protocol for handling player gripes. The exact words exchanged, between the two, were never revealed. At least as far as we know, Lajoie did not slam a chair over the head of Birmingham, as Stovall had done to him.

Lajoie then could hold a grudge. When asked by the president of the North Atlantic League to comeback to baseball and manage his Syracuse Stars team, Lajoie gave two reasons for turning down the offer. "I hate the sound of locomotive whistles. Second, you had a ballplayer who you released. If he was still with you, I'd manage the Stars, but I wouldn't release him, I'd kill him."

There might then have been some Cobb in Lajoie.

CHAPTER FIFTEEN

"I am a Baseball Player, Not a Talker"

The New England Patriot beat reporter hoped against hope that Bill Belichick would reveal his reasoning behind some curious coaching decisions that day. They seemed to suggest some hidden logic related to playoff positioning:

"Does home advantage really mean anything, Coach?"

"It is what it is. Whoever we play, we play. We just have to do a better job of coaching and playing."

There was to be no follow up. As usual, darkness filled the press room.

The raging popularity of baseball brought with it an insatiable demand to learn everything possible about the heroes of the diamond. It seems 1908 was a watershed year. "Take Me Out to the Ball Game" was published in 1908. In 1908, the sports page made its first appearance in American newspapers. In 1908 as well, the Baseball Writers Association was formed. They were soon a force to be reckoned with. By 1937, they were part of the formidable fraternity who cast the first Hall of Fame ballots.

In ceremonial situations, Lajoie could be particularly anxious. Even in front of Woonsocket and Cleveland gatherings of friends, he tried to make it short and sweet. His Hall of Fame induction speech was over in less than a minute. The brevity of his remarks was often attributed to his humility, and indeed that was a part. Toastmasters knew not to expect Larry to be at the podium for long. In informal settings-the baseball or golf clubhouse with friends, the dinner table with friends and family, etc.; it was a different matter, and Larry could hold court with best of them. He both loved telling and listening to the tales of the game.

In general, however, no matter what the venue, he did not like talking about himself, held many things close to the chest. He also was uncomfortable with being an object of public scrutiny or being considered authoritative voice on baseball matters or happenings. As he succinctly put it, "I am a baseball player, not a talker."

• • •

As might be expected, this reticence did not endear him to the swelling ranks who made a living spreading baseball chatter and squeezing out the last ounce of verbiage to a hero worshipping mob of bugs and cranks. No doubt New England Patriots Coach Bill Belichick would have understood Lajoie's priorities. In his own way, Belichick too begins a press conference with "I am a football coach, not a talker" disclaimer. While not as sullen as Bill Belichick, Lajoie too gave the impression that reporters were to be tolerated at best. He knew they had a job to do and generally felt they were "nice enough fellows," but he had no intention of being their plaything. In fact, Mr. Belichick might learn from Nap a few techniques to keep reporters at bay and frustrated. For instance, on one occasion, Lajoie stated the time limits for questions and held reporters to them: "Go ahead. I'll give you five minutes. One to ask questions and I will answer in four.' He could also control content of the interview: "No, I won't tell you the story of my life." He also often dismissed follow- up questions. On other occasions, he would predict their questions, armed with responses intended to spare him the ordeal of the same old, same old. The logic was to anticipate the question, answer it to his liking, and render the reporter impotent. A few cases in point:

> Do I earn my $7,000 a year?
> Response: Ask the Cleveland club.

> What made you become a player?
> Response: I needed the money

> How do I play?
> Response: Go out to the ball park and see for yourself.

> What balls do I like best?
> Response: Ones I can't reach.

Where do I like to hit the ball?
Response: Over the fence.

What other places?
Response: Where the fielders aren't standing.

What do I do with my money?
Response: Give it to Standard Oil. They need it.

Why was I named Napoleon?
Response: My parents wanted me to at least have a famous name.

When he wasn't posing as his own interviewer, his answers could be brief and elaboration non-existent. Delivered with twinkling-eyed humor or the straightforward sincerity of common sense, his answers said it all or said nothing, depending on what clothes the Emperor wore or didn't. The following responses show that he could be a smart ass, of sorts.

What is the secret of being a great hitter?
Response: Hit the ball.

What is the secret to your marvelous fielding?
Response: I just move along and grab the ball if I can.

How do you explain why you cover so much ground at second?
Response: I don't know anything about it than this. I have big feet.

Asked to explain the strategy of hitting, Lajoie responded: "When a man is eating, he doesn't have to stop as he does to ask himself,

'How high should I hold the fork at every bit or how wide should I open my mouth?'"

This dislike of making things appear more complicated that they were did not only emerge when discussing baseball. Asked to explain how through 18 holes he had missed but one putt, a 15 footer, Lajoie responded, "Why fool around the hole That's the ball. There's the hole. What else is there but to tap it in?"

There were no secrets to be guarded. Ty Cobb was the Mason, not he.

All this was not aimed necessarily at frustrating the press. It was not meant necessarily to intentionally obfuscate things. It was not part of a vendetta against the press concocted by a disgusted Ted Williams. Lajoie had no such antipathy towards anyone unless his pride and integrity had been questioned. Part of it was his nature. For one thing, he was determined not to complicate things, not to build professorial towers or priestly pulpits.

"Father Lajoie, how does one get into Heaven?" Open the gate, my son.

In any case, at times Lajoie's banter was playful posturing, while at other times it reflected annoyance. Lajoie was having a good time, nevertheless. He brought an entire entertaining arsenal to play, from a Will Rogers-like mix of everyday analogies and common sense observations, to dry wit, to sarcasm. Bottom line was that the big footed Lajoie enjoyed the cat and mouse game and had the sense of humor to pull it off.

Because he could choose not to play their game at all or could choose to beat them at their own game, Lajoie was not that popular with the press. There were exceptions, including Grantland Rice and a few favored writers like Jimmy Powers and Arthur Daley. Cobb, McGraw,

Wagner then were the ones to interview. Lajoie shed no tears, made no dramatic attempts to keep his limelight from dimming. In the last few decades of his life, he was interviewed with some regularity by the *Sporting News*. In fact, he remained an ardent reader of the paper; at least a few photos show him in his rocking chair, pipe in place as he read headlines. This was during his retirement, of course, when he began to be comfortable with being a retrospective voice of the game as it was once played. During his playing days, however, he felt harangued by fame and so even when reporters found their way to his refuge-the farm- he managed to multi task, answering questions while tossing feed to the chicken or grooming his horses Polly and Molly. Of course, the chickens and horses and pigs came first and the reporters could always be fed leftovers.

Some conjecture:

And how would Ted Williams, the guru of how to hit and how to fish, and Napoleon Lajoie have gotten along? Ted's constant criticism of the hitting techniques and knowledge of his Red Sox teammates could be annoying. Bobby Doerr, Dom DiMaggio, Johnny Pesky and the others, having heard the constant stream of pontification aimed at their hitting style and approaches, learned not to get defensive, not be jock-eyed. The quartet remained life-long friends with each other, with Ted as their lynchpin. If Lajoie had been asked by Ted to expound on the art of fishing? His response would have been predictable: "Why fool around? There's the bait? There's the line. There's the water. What else is there to do but throw it in?" And who soon also would have been thrown into that water? The Splendid Splinter. He would have had no chance against a big Frenchman who was not about to be lectured to and was hungry.

CHAPTER SIXTEEN

A Race with No Winner

A bride may try on the wedding dress, but she doesn't have her photos taken until the wedding day.

Ken Griffey, Jr. doesn't visit the Hall of Fame until he has been voted in (Griffey, Jr. was to received 99.3 % of the votes, highest in history).

Neither Ty Cobb nor Napoleon Lajoie could be coerced into sitting behind the wheel of the Chalmers 33, the automobile to be awarded to the players in each league with the highest average. The National League contest for such was already a done deal, not so for the Junior

Circuit. Cobb and Lajoie were within points of each other. Nothing had been decided yet. It was presumptuous to assume victory. To do so might invite bad luck. Unwilling to give the other man an advantage, they sat together in the back seat.

The nation was obsessed with it all. For one thing, an automobile was quite the prize. There were only 8,000 automobiles on the road and only 1 of 200 eligible drivers had one. For another thing, the pennant race in the American League that year had never materialized and so the battle between the aging superstar Lajoie (now 35) and the incomparable twenty-three year old Cobb became high drama. The personalities of the combatants could not have been more different and the sympathies of the nation more unanimous. In one corner- Lajoie- the "how could you not like the guy?" favorite of fans and players. In the other, Cobb- the "meaner than the devil" man, the darling only of Lucifer and his cohorts. It was in many ways the first and only time the two superstars were highlighted as direct adversaries, appearing side by side in every paper every week. It was the first and last time that a fan would look up the average of one to determine where he stood in relation to the other.

The race went until the last game of the season. In the end, Cobb would win and Lajoie would lose. In the end, both would win, but Lajoie no longer wanted the prize. In the end, Lajoie would win a pyrrhic victory. In the end, the man in the center of a supposed cheating controversy might have been cheated. Okay, time to explain all this mystic mummery.

The drama had its up's and down's, but for three months each was in reach of the other. The battle was a classic of punch and counterpunch. By August's end, Cobb had a three-point lead. In the first half of September, Lajoie hit at a .377 clip, Cobb at .412 but with far fewer at-bats. In the second half of the month, Cobb hit .492, Lajoie .360. Complicating everything was that official and non-official figures were everywhere, collected by a host of statisticians and representing different time frames. In effect, going into October, no one could say with certainty who had the lead. Detroit and Cleveland went head to head in a doubleheader. Each man went 3 for 6. Two games remained.

Cobb sat out those final two games. One theory is that he had another bout with a reoccurring eye problem. A Cleveland paper doubted the truth of that theory claiming that in reality Cobb was suffering from "congealed condition of *pedal extremitis* -- cold feet." The other explanation given is that under the impression that he had an insurmountable lead going into those games, Cobb saw no need to jeopardize things. Ty's security might not have been on target. One set of figures showed Lajoie in the lead by four points going into the final two games. In either scenario, Cobb did leave the team and stories spread that Ty had slipped off to see a Broadway play. Lajoie went to St Louis to star in his own drama.

In the season ending doubleheader, necessitated by a previous game rain out, Lajoie went 8 for 8. First hit was a triple. Six were bunts down third base to a rookie third baseman who had been ordered by his manager to play exceptionally deep, ridiculously deep. It appeared that Lajoie was to be the winner. In a testimony to Cobb's disfavor among his teammates, members of the Tigers telegraphed congratulations to Lajoie. In fact, many managers ordered their third baseman to play deep when Lajoie came to bat, allow the bunt hit rather risk the murderous line drive. Such was Connie Mack's strategy. After playing up close and successfully throwing out Lajoie on a bunt attempt, Home Run Baker ,nevertheless, was confronted by an irate Mack who again warned him of the consequences of facing" the buzz saw" that was a Lajoie line drive. Of course, even Mack would not have asked his player to retreat almost to the outfield grass as did manager O'Conner that day.

Many smelled a rat. The conspiracy theory was fairly simple. Brown's manager O'Conner hated Cobb and had enacted his revenge. According to the theory, O'Conner's contention that his playing his third baseman so deep was a judicious concession to Lajoie's notoriously brutal shots down third base was hogwash. In addition, since the players on both teams, all teams, most of the fans across the country, and the grand majority of those who now or once held a glove disliked Cobb, the victory would be that much sweeter. Rumors about unsavory behaviors flew. One that Brown's coach Howell had made frequent visit to the scorekeeper to check if the bunts were indeed credited as hits, not errors. In one at-bat, a sacrifice in which Lajoie beat the throw, he was not given a hit. A note was passed to the official supposedly offering him a small bribe (a new suit?) "to do well by Lajoie" on the sacrifice ruling. Lajoie himself admitted to having telephoned the official scorer to determine if he had been awarded that ninth hit, claiming that even Umpire Evans agreed with him. Explaining the six bunts hits, Lajoie's commented, "After that triple, they expected powerful swings. I fooled them right along."

A few days later, third baseman Corriden made his safety-first defense saying that "I want to remain in baseball for some years. I might have gotten to some of those bunts and at the same time broken a nose or lost a few teeth."

Told that Detroit owner Navin was suspicious, Lajoie shot back, "Well he knows what he can do, and if he takes it before the league, I will have my say." President Ban Johnson did investigate, interviewing manager, third baseman and coach of the Brown, not Lajoie. O'Connor was banned from baseball, although he successfully sued for his 1911 salary. Corriden was cleared, Howell was also banned from baseball.

Cleared of any collusion, his integrity now not an issue, Lajoie admitted that "the players were in my corner at any rate. They didn't try any too hard to get me out." Such was a very reasonable premise.

Cobb took the high road. "I am sorry that either Lajoie or I did not win the prize without anything occurring that could cause unfavorable comment." To his credit, over the long wait before the decision was announced, Cobb refused to lobby for himself or play the wronged victim. In fact, during the entire title battle, the usually combative Cobb rarely if ever argued with official scorers. It wasn't until early November that the final results were announced and Cobb pronounced the winner by a percentage point, .385 to .384.

One of the stranger events associated with the American League's investigation was Johnson's decision to order a check of Cobb's official batting average. In 1981, the Sporting News did its own review, including examining copies of the official A.L. scoring sheets. In that review it was clear that the American League statistician had mistakenly entered the Detroit figures for the second game of a September 24th doubleheader as the second game on September 25, a day in which

● ● ●

the Tigers had played but a single game. Finding the second game of September 24th missing, the line was repeated as a September 24 game. The consequence of all the additions was that Cobb twice got credit for his 2-for-3 performance in the second game on September 24th. Finding it as "curious" that on the sheets there were "cross outs of the extra game entry for every Detroit player except Cobb," the News asked, "Were Cobb's extra hits retained by order of Ban Johnson? That is not known." The *Sporting News* revised tabulations, which included revision in Lajoie statistics as well, showed Lajoie to be the winner by fractions of a point.

Johnson's report certified Ty's "clear title" to the batting championship. In that same report, Johnson revealed that he had made an offer to purchase a duplicate car for Lajoie in recognition of his great service to the American League and his grand season. Mr. Chalmers asked if he could do the honor and Johnson acceded. It seemed that Johnson's overriding purpose was to keep the two jewels in the American League crown happy.

The dust cleared. The Chalmers Company officials smiled. The publicity gained more than outweighed the cost of the extra automobile. Theirs was a brilliant piece of sports marketing. Cobb smiled. His streak of 4 consecutive batting titles was still alive, eventually to reach six. The next year he won another car. The league smiled. However controversial a poster child, Ty Cobb continued his remarkable achievements, name a player in the National League who was so well known. It was not to be the first time that Ban Johnson seemed intent on preserving the brilliance of Cobb. In 1922, he overruled an official scorer's designation of an error and Ty's average climbed from .398 to .401, his third .400 season. Napoleon Lajoie did not smile. Publically, he brushed it off saying that he was told that the car they gave him ran a lot better than the one given to Ty. Most likely, Nap's nephew told the real story. Lionel Lajoie contended that his uncle, "was given a Chalmers car, but he

didn't want to accept it. It was Myrtle who made him accept it. He just
thought that he, not Cobb should have won that championship and was
angry that Cobb had been ruled the winner." Such a reaction is in character for Lajoie. When informed that his 1901 season average was to be
raised from .405 to .422 because later research discovered he had not
been credited with nine hits, Lajoie remarked tenaciously, "Those hits
belong to me. I am glad they found them." With the extra points, Lajoie
surpassed Ty Cobb's highest season average, .412. Perhaps, that was
some compensation for 1910.

Lajoie's reaction to losing the batting championship might have
had a little to do with the Cobb-Lajoie competition. After all, a fading
superstar would have liked to have been the reigning king one more
time, and an opportunity to derail the Cobb express would be satisfying.
It might have been a little about adding another legacy jewel, another
batting crown. It was much about the perceived injustice of it all. Lajoie
felt he had been cheated. He had earned the award. *The Sporting News*
agreed and sent its case to Commissioner Kuhn. Kuhn rejected it, citing
statute of limitation reasoning. The *News* noted that 21 revisions in the
record of Hall of Famer Tris Speaker had sailed by the revision committee the previous year. American League President, Phil MacPhail agreed
with Kuhn saying that, "Unless we examine all the records completely,
we shouldn't change only this one." The *News* countered that such was
not the case when Babe Ruth's RBI totals and Walter Johnson's ERA totals were revised. The News concluded that, "After 70 years, the odor
may linger over Lajoie's seven bunts, but the questions over Cobb's
phantom 2-for-3 are larger."

Lajoie might as well have sat behind the wheel that day.

CHAPTER SEVENTEEN

Less Is More

We were rough and ready guys, but oh, how we could harmonize. Heart of my Heart, bring back those memories."
> --Heart of My Heart, 1923

U pon returning to the bench after committing his fifth error of the game, a downtrodden Lajoie was approached by a tall and thin man wearing a derby. Tapping Lajoie on the shoulder, he offered consolation. "Stick with it long enough, and you'll get one." If such a remark had been said by anyone else but the venerable Mack, fists might have flown. The fifth error put Lajoie in the record books for most errors committed by as second baseman in a game.

Napoleon had returned to Connie Mack to play for his Philadelphia A's. The reunion with Connie had been rewarding; Connie even had come to Napoleon's home to recruit him. Soon after signing, Lajoie admitted that he did so with the hope that with Mr. Mack he might finally be able to win that elusive league championship. The Philly papers were not so sure, one of them afraid that the Mackmen's six consecutive league championships might end with the addition of the jinx-pursued Lajoie.

It did.

Lajoie knew that the handwriting was on the wall. It wasn't only that the great connect between coordination and execution had fallen apart, that desire and execution now slept in separate beds, both at home and on the road. After 24 years, he wanted a reprieve from it all, the grind of travel, the know-it-all fans, and the time away from wife and farm. Even the sound of train whistles and bells was wearying. The game for the moment at least had lost its romance, even for him. Enough was enough.

The photo taken outside of the Cleveland Naps hotel over a decade earlier shows a different Lajoie. He seems to be holding court, surrounded by joking teammates, men who shared rooms and sleeping berths, often ate together, played poker together, and played practical jokes on each other and others. The quiet center of it all, Lajoie appears preoccupied, the picture of contentment.

And what was he thinking about as he puffed away with such seeming serenity? A thousand stories were suspended in the smoke ready to be inhaled for safe keeping when the night got dark too early.

Maybe it was about the time he and a few mates had pretended to be delegates to the political convention that had swept into Cleveland

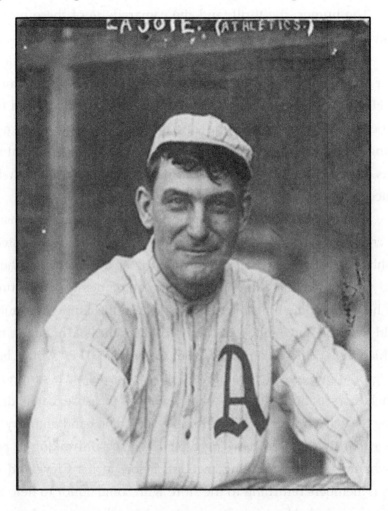

town. The looks they got when they espoused secret Democratic allegiance to the Republicans gathered and vice-a versa. Or the look on "Wee Willy" Keeler's face when he looked up to be greeted by a Lajoie line drive that hit him on the chest and toppled him like a deck of cards. When an irate and embarrassed Wee Willy arrived at second later in the game, the little guy wasn't afraid to drive a few words into the chest of the Gulliver standing at the base and aim his spikes at his shins. *Hadda' like that guy.*

The humor, the thrill, and the camaraderie of these moments would always be bathed in soft light.

The cigar in the photo was not a prop. After all, Lajoie was part owner of a cigar store in Cleveland. Smoking remained a habit until the end. His pipe was a constant companion in retirement, a portal to the past perhaps. Photos of Larry mowing the lawn, of lifting a pick axe, of reading his beloved *Sporting News,* all have him brandishing that ubiquitous pipe. No doubt he emerged from such activity to tell his wife or his niece about *"the time when."*

It would be easy to Photoshop the photo for public consumption, create a brash, cigar smoking figure with a hat that suggested his swashbuckling heritage. Raising himself up, the d'Artagnan of the Diamond puffing one last time on that cigar, announcing, "Boys, time to raise hell." Or something like that. No doubt the Emperor's minions would willingly have followed him into the arenas of the night, many of which they could recommend from experience. They would be following in a long tradition of players who followed such summons to brothels, bars, dance halls, and other venues of pleasure. Lajoie did not belong to such a fraternity of hell raisers. He led no band of merry men. He was hardly the hard partying type. Even social drinking in public was shunned. A fan recalling meeting Lajoie at his Cleveland cigar store, remembers returning to the store with some liquor to help enjoy the music provided by a jazz band entertaining the patrons. Lajoie was there at the time, rather nattily dressed in his Prince Albert coat. Offered a drink by the fan, Lajoie politely declined the invite and moved off into the shadows. Forty years later the adoring fan remembered that evening and spoke of the dignity of Lajoie.

The usual evening for Lajoie ended early, preceded by a hotel meal, and some socialization with a player or two or a friend who might have dropped by the hotel. That friend's suggestion that they take in a movie would be declined; movies hurt the eyes and eyes were a ballplayer's meal ticket. Anyway, he had homework to do, managerial decisions to be pondered. The job had to be done to the best of his abilities. Managerial responsibilities accomplished, time to fall asleep to a good book or to a newspaper sports page? No. Again, reading hurt the eyes.

As much as his resignation as player manager would relieve him from managerial angst and spark a renaissance of his hitting and fielding performances the very next year, Lajoie was not by nature a worry wart constantly putting pins in himself. After a few tosses with the pillow, he fell asleep. It isn't too far-fetched to think that sentimental and nostalgic Lajoie fell asleep while staring at the canvas sneakers he carried with him even on the road, the ones he had worn when playing for Fall River twenty years earlier.

Ah, Fall River. I wonder how Artie Butler is doing? That man could play...

A man about town, a social butterfly, Lajoie wasn't and never would be. "He is not what they call a good fellow, never one of the boys," offered a writer who knew him well. "At home or on tour," continued the writer, "he would take friends one at a time for supper or for a quiet chat and smoke." On the road on occasion, Lajoie allowed himself a trip to friends in whatever city the team was visiting. If in Cleveland, he might take a jaunt to the theater with Mrs. Lajoie,. Of course, none of these frivolities on game nights. During the off season was a slightly different story, but he was not a social mixer, preferring to do what talking he did to small numbers of known friends. In some ways, he was still the socially awkward hayseed described by Hapgood when Lajoie first traveled to Boston. He remained for his entire life a person who was most comfortable in familiar places with a few familiar people. His own cocoon.

There was nothing morose about Lajoie, and since he didn't take himself so seriously, he had no self-important airs. He could have fun. He could assume "the Frenchie from Woonsocket/Fall River" dialect. He could obligingly embarrass himself as when he agreed to wear a skirt over his uniform all for an inane caption that read, "Lajoie endures the batting handicap of wearing a long skirt that came down to his feet."

Unlike Cobb, he also could indulge in the horseplay and the comic relief vital to a team and his own sanity. During a training camp trip in 1910, while sitting in the stands with his teammates Bradley and Bemis, Lajoie was accosted by a fan who asked "Lajoie is with this team isn't he?"

"Yes," Lajoie replied. The game was on.

"Great player, isn't he?"

"Used to be" chimed in Bradley. "Gone back a lot. Slowed up so much he can hardly get out of his way. Eyes are bad too, but he has been lucky with the bat. Just shuts his eyes and swings."

The duped fan shifted his attention. "Well, Bradley is a wonderful third baseman. Isn't he?" he asked.

"Whoever told you that, "interrupted Lajoie, "must have been stringing you. He is one of the most overrated players in the big leagues. He must have a stand-in with manager to hold his job. Where he belongs is in a circus. As a third baseman, he's a clown."

"That's what I always thought, "retorted the fan. "I have seen Bradley and Lajoie play lots of times and always thought they were four-flushers. Down in Corsicana, we have boys on the lots who could do better."

"Don't know about that," responded Bradley. "This man Bradley isn't so bad, but when you say that Lajoie is a four-flusher, you hit about right."

Not to be out done, Lajoie remarked," What are you talking about? There are a dozen third baseman in the big show better than Bradley."

"Well," said the confident fan, "if you want to know my honest opinion- and I am a man who has watched them play all over the country- I think both of them are overpaid."

Their ruse accomplished, Lajoie and his mates moved away towards the playing field. When the players were out of ear shot, the fan asked the writer, "Those two men belong to the Cleveland club, don't they? Who are they?"

"Bradley and Lajoie," said the straight faced writer.

Lajoie was a good-hearted and good-natured French Canadian according to one writer. To another, he was a boy with that twinkle in his eye, always joking with players and strangers, his popularity among the players again stemming from "his refusal to take himself seriously." In *Glory of Their Times*, Tommy Leach offers a similar perspective, one that seemed to be shared by many fellow players. "What a ballplayer that man was…. He was a pleasure to play against too, always laughing and joking. Even when the son of a gun was blocking you off the base, he was smiling and kidding with you. You just had to like the guy."

Sounds like a Big Papi figure, seizing upon his arrival at a base as an opportunity to socialize and chatter.

And Cobb?

None doubted that he played the game ferociously. Some thought he was a dark comic trickster; if there are fifty ways to leave

Spring training, Georgia. Fun in the sun.

your lover, Cobb had sixteen ways to steal a base. And when he arrived at second, taken what you thought was yours, he gloated. There was no time to socialize for he was plotting to steal your underwear for all to see.

Few players had more confrontations on the field with Cobb than Cy Young. The Cy Young and Cobb field relationship was a stream of obscenities and brush back pitches. "Cobb is going at it too hard," said Young, suggesting the joylessness of being Cobb.

Empathy aside, however, most players thought Ty the guy "you just had to hate." This difference in popularity between the two superstars might have explained why so many players, including his own teammates, wanted Lajoie, not Cobb, to win that automobile.

Having Some Fun with "The Controversy"

abridged from a 1910 Canadian newspaper

National Baseball Commission chair Herrmann strikes his gavel:

Herrmann: Mr. Cobb, tell the Committee what happened on September 7, 1910.
Cobb: I was suddenly seized with eye trouble. Doctors called it cyclitis. couldn't see.
Herrmann: Couldn't see what?
Cobb: Couldn't see that I could lose that automobile if I stood pat.
Herrmann: How long did this cyclitis last?
Cobb: Until September 21. I suddenly could see again.
Herrmann: See what?
Cobb: See my finish. I got back in the game.
Herrmann: For how long?
Cobb: Until October 9, 1910.
Herrmann: What happened then?
Cobb: I again was struck with the dreaded disease.
Hermann: What was your average then? And Mr. Lajoie's?
Cobb: Mine was .382. His was .378.
Herrmann: That is enough. Call Mr. Lajoie. (Lajoie takes the stand) What is your name?
Lajoie: Napoleon Lajoie, sir.
Herrmann: Any relation to the second fiddle at Waterloo?
Lajoie: He was a cousin of mine.
Herrmann: You are commonly called *Larry*, are you not? Why?
Lajoie: Because my name is Napoleon.
Herrmann: Is it not fact that in baseball you are known as a heavy hitter? How then do you account for the fact that on October 9, 1910, you lay down seven straight bunts and got away with six of them?
Lajoie: I have always made it a tradition in my long and honored career that when the 9th of a month falls on Sunday I resort to the bunt.
Herrmann: Next. Mr. O'Connor come forth. I want you to answer this question with perfect honesty. Do you think any member of your team is capable of playing dishonest ball?
O'Connor (with earnestness): I don't think any member of my team is capable of playing any kind of ball.
Herrmann: Next witness, Mr. Corriden.
Herrmann: Mr.Corriden what do you say to the charge that you deliberately played too far back at third so as to allow Mr. Lajoie to achieve six bunt hits?
Corriden: I was suddenly seized with an affliction of the foot the doctors called pedalitis. In excruciating pain from the hard ground of the infield, I was forced to retreat to the soft yielding turf behind third. Otherwise I would have fallen in my tracks and been accused of lying down. See?
Herrmann: I do.

The court decided that the automobile should be awarded to neither player.

CHAPTER EIGHTEEN

End Games

I save my praise for only the best.
So you can take your homers and your hot dogs
But give me Napoleon Lajoie.
-- Ty Cobb

As much as Cobb esteemed Lajoie, there is no doubt that his comment was part of long anti-Ruth campaign waged against the man who had dethroned him. That Ruth had dethroned him was part of the equation. Richard Bak targeted the reason for the antagonism, explaining that Ruth was "flypaper for all that was wrong in the game." To Cobb, baseball's worship of the home run was wrong, and its abandonment of strategy was wrong. In addition, Ruth's galling lack of discipline at the plate was symptomatic of baseball's decline. Finally, Cobb felt that Ruth's off-the-field antics were an embarrassing effrontery to the game. Answering those who at this point might call Cobb out for being a hypocrite, Bak reminds us that Ruth was no choir boy. In one season alone, he was suspended four times. He showed his lack of repentance by being suspended five times the next year. Like Cobb, he would charge into the stands after hecklers, albeit with less murderous intent. He punched umpires and bullied managers and lead the

Don't be fooled by the seeming civility.

charge to his favorite brothel, The House of the Good Shephard in St. Louis. At least three paternity suits were served against him. Every majestic home run must have brought forgiving rain for the nation winked at the indiscretions of the man-child.

The Ruth-Cobb hostility came to a head when, upon Manager Cobb's orders, a bean ball narrowly missed Ruth's head and a fastball landed squarely in the next batter's back. As fights broke out at various locations, one report had it that Cobb and Ruth headed straight for each other, "plowing into each other like runaway trains." After Ruth's retirement, things settled down between the two. The fact that Cobb was the number one vote getter for the Hall of Fame, outpolling Ruth by 7 votes, may have provided Cobb with the ballast needed to seek peaceful co-existence. Unfortunately, he did not find such ballast elsewhere.

Building close mutual relationships was for Cobb more difficult that placing a perfect bunt. That Ty's first marriage to a seventeen-year-old Georgia girl lasted over thirty years was a tribute to her forbearance. Mentioning that she had spent time in a convent, a writer pronounced her a strong candidate for sainthood for putting up with Ty's abuses. According to family members, she was beaten by Cobb on a few occasions, once with a baseball bat. When Ty came home, his children scattered in fear. As adults, they thought their life good if he was not a part of it. And yet, children were dear to his heart as reflected in his frequent appearance at Shriners' events for handicapped children and in his establishment of a well-endowed fund for disadvantaged children in Georgia. It was intimacy that he could not master. After three aborted divorce filings, Charlie Cobb finally had had enough of his anger, domination, and drinking. Two years later, Cobb remarried. The marriage lasted seven years. His wife said that she was physically afraid of her husband. After the divorce, living alone in Atherton, CA., he moved back in 1959 to an equally empty house in Royston, Georgia. By his own admission, he was "a lonely old man."

Meanwhile, modern baseball's first superstar, the most essential of the founding fathers who took the field to establish the American League's turf, the player who took on the reserve clause, who played against the greatest player of his (all) time and won his esteem, who won the first Triple Crown with an average which is still the highest average in American League history, who garnered more Hall of Fame votes than Cy Young, conducted his public and private affairs without fanfare.

A pipe, a Sporting News, a rocking chair and a wealth of memories.

At 27, Napoleon Lajoie married a divorcee, Myrtle Smith. The childless marriage lasted over forty years. They were uncomplicated years of tranquility and ease. In off-season, Lajoie worked the farm in

Dogs were a constant source of entertainment and companionship for Nap.

There were lighter moments to be shared with Jimmie Foxx.

Mentor. In retirement, the Lajoies were ensconced in Florida from 1940 on, at first a rental and then a home. Lajoie mowed the lawn, handled the pick axe, helped in chores inside and out, and added letters and articles to his scrapbooks. Death continued to collect his own keepsakes as well. Upon Myrtle's death in 1954, Nap's five brothers and two sisters were all dead. Nap's niece and her husband sold their Woonsocket furniture store and came down to care for "our Uncle Larry." They found him appreciative, humble and nostalgic. The good natured Frenchman had lost none of his geniality and was still the most handsome guy on the block.

While every day Cobb added to his list of the son-of-the-bitches who he said had it out for him, Larry invited ex-ball players and Woonsocket friends to his home to talk of "those days." Indeed, more than a few reporters and friends were told that they "better not forget to stop by" when they next traveled through Holly Hill. They did not forget. From the local sports writer from Woonsocket and Fall River or small city outside of Boston to the New York celebrity writers, they came and looked forward to the next visit.

While Cobb traveled to Keith, Scotland to talk to bird hunting's finest shotgun artists, Lajoie traveled down the road to enter his roosters in local competitions and learn from local farmers, many of whom had never left the state. While Ty took his defense of the game and of himself on the road, twice appearing in *Life Magazine*, Lajoie stood behind the left field fence watching Little League games,

Nap found many ways to keep in shape. Each ended in a smoke.

joking that his new job was "signing autographs for the kids, a job I enjoyed very much." The mail brought on average twenty fan letters a day and the latest *Sporting News*, which on occasion featured articles about the Emperor of the Diamond. In fairness to Cobb, he too assiduously signed the many autograph requests that came his way.

While in his final years, Cobb's withering body became the host for raging cancer, diabetes, and high blood pressure, Lajoie remained healthy until the very end. Even into Lajoie's late seventies, returning visitors to Lillian and Napoleon's home spoke unerringly of how erect *old Nap* stood, how strong was his handshake, and how gracious he was to them. In the spring of 1957, Nap was seduced to attend an exhibition game between the Cleveland Indians and the New York Giants as part of celebration of Nap Lajoie Day in Daytona Beach. On that day, "82 and still erect, he strode to the mound and pitched the first ball as 3,500 fans went wild." Stricken with pneumonia in January of 1959, he died in February. Little Leaguers from the Daytona Little League were the honor guard for their honorary league president. An ex-Giant catcher, Grover Land, was one of the pallbearers. No baseball notables attended the service. No Hall of Fame officials came. A floral bat was sent. It had been

Still robust in his sixties and wintering in Florida,
Nap tries his hand at bocce and mows his lawn.

a long time since the umpire had walked in front of the grandstands and cried out the name of Napoleon Lajoie, and it was time to join Addie Joss. Upon his death, his niece wrote the following to a friend:

> *...Having lost Uncle Larry makes the house seem real empty. Both my husband and myself felt that he was more a father than an uncle. We shared a closeness that makes us proud. It's a good feeling to know that he was very happy with us. It was a great honor for us to be with him...*

After a protracted battle with prostate cancer, a lonely Ty Cobb died in 1961 in Emory Hospital, Georgia. A few ex-players attended the funeral, as did the director of the Hall of Fame. After reading Al Stump's biography on Cobb, Roger Kahn, author of *The Boys of Summer*, proclaimed: "It is Cobb in his last days -- defiant, angry, drunken, prayerful, desperate to be remembered -- that is so haunting, and so memorable and so terrifying." A few days before his death, Cobb sent

March 19-1959.

Dear Mr. Bissell:

We gratefully acknowledge your kind letter to us at this time.

Having lost Uncle Larry makes the house seem real empty. Both my husband and myself felt that he was more a "Father" than "Uncle". We shared a closeness that makes us so proud. Its a good feeling to know

Stump a photo of the family mausoleum. Across the photo was written "Any Day Now." On his bedside table were a million dollars of negotiable securities. On top of them, his luger. God knows what confrontations a delirious Cobb might have imagined. The list must have been long, but best guess is that, even in the afterlife, Commissioner Keneshaw Landis would be well advised to wear catchers' shin protectors, at the least. For Cobb's sake, it would have been nice if the often-folded letter from his father written sixty years ago had been on that bedside. That would have allowed writers to humanize Cobb. To speak of his crying at the mausoleum he built for his parents. Of his successful campaign to get former teammate Heilman into the Hall of Fame, whispering into the ear of the dying teammate that had been elected (election would be months later). Of his $200 gift to the Addie Joss family. Unable to rehabilitate himself, it never dawned on him he could leave behind props that nevertheless would allow for some rewriting of the script.

Published after his death, his sanitized autobiography, *My Life in Baseball-the True Record,* had been an attempt to rewrite that script, to set the record straight but the ghostwriter of that book, Al Stump, decided years later to again set the record straight. His book's sub-title read: "The life and times of the meanest man who ever played baseball."

However much still in the grasp of demons, Cobb did not wander off the human reservation in his final years. His nurse said that his greatest wish was just to be remembered, a prayer most of us mumble as we seek dual citizenship on earth and heaven. In addition, as the years advanced, he admitted that he missed many of those with whom he played. Otherwise contented, Lajoie, also spoke of the same

Ty's battle with cancer was just beginning.
He was the last of the nine from the original Hall of Fame class. to die.

pervading sadness. "I sit here on my front porch. I like to smoke my pipe and think of the days when baseball was my life. There aren't many players left who can talk to me about the players I knew."

Cobb and Lajoie then were no different that the men who gather under the lights in the parking lot in the early evening and talk of that year they played for the state championship and the tantalizing "how close we came" soon becomes "what a character that guy was!" or "how did you ever catch that ball?" And one summer, there are only two of you to tell the stories, even if one is imaginary. We all have ghostly imaginations in service to preserving and creating who we were.

To both Cobb and Lajoie, the game was a final resting spot, a clean well-lighted place. It was not about friendships brought from that field. It was being on that field together. And thus two men who were never friends could find reason to be together.

On a warm July day in Florida, the still tormented renegade came to the tranquil homesteader. He expected a gracious welcome. During and after his career, Napoleon Lajoie had expressed no ill will against the man who had taken his throne, who had dressed in his uniform, who had won his batting crown and automobile, and who had taken his spotlight.

Perhaps Lajoie understood that Cobb was a feral cat. Even as the inviting warmth of the lighted house poured through an open door, Cobb retreated into the cold, howling night he had created. He had no choice, really. Putting on his canvas sneakers from his first professional game at Fall River and grabbing his gold tipped cane from the grateful citizens of Woonsocket, Napoleon Lajoie walked out into the daylight he had created. He was in the shadow of no man, and he surely would not have wanted to change places with anyone.

EPILOGUE

I am sending to you the pipe that Uncle Larry enjoyed mostly while rocking in his favorite chair on the porch. If it could talk this little pipe would have quite a story. It heard many old ball players talking over old times, laughing at some little jokes, and just visiting."

-- Lilian Lajoie Lamoureux, Holly Hills, Florida, March, 1959

Men who had become political enemies during their political careers, Thomas Jefferson and John Adams began a retirement correspondence that included 156 letters. According to Adams, their professed purpose in writing to each other was "not to die without first having explained ourselves to each other." Ironically, they died on the same day, that day being the Fourth of July.

Ty Cobb and Napoleon Lajoie had no need to reconcile; neither in their playing days nor in their retirement years was their relationship filled with enmity nor distrust. In addition, they had no reason nor inclination to create intimacies. They were not friends. Few players were Ty Cobb's friend. According to one baseball historian, Cobb was "as welcomed as a mosquito in the bedroom." Many disliked him, a few hated him, and most were wary of approaching or disturbing him. Cobb himself made clear the guidelines for any attempts to approach him. He declared that those who wanted to spend time with him had better not "increase my tension." That tension was always at threshold. Lajoie was too proud and stubborn to find such subordination appealing.

Retirement provided opportunities for each man to indulge their inclinations. Ty spent years explaining himself to the public, trying to erase what he saw as misunderstanding of his ways and motivations. "There are several false lights that I have been placed in that I feel an urge to correct," Cobb told a potential autobiography collaborator. In

1960, work began on an autobiography which according to Cobb would "set the record straight." Cobb never got to read *My Life in Baseball, The True Story*. He died three months before its publication in August, 1961. Lajoie felt no overbearing need to explain himself to anyone, to set some record straight. However much as he avoided center stage, his dry wit and welcoming ways entertained all who sought him out.

Both Cobb and Lajoie, however, both saw themselves as "defenders of the faith." Each frequently spoke of the superiority of the game of baseball as it was played and understood in their time. Each cherished its gladiatorial mentality.

Perhaps it was fraternity that brought Ty Cobb to Holly Hills, Florida to visit Napoleon Lajoie on that warm July day in 1956. Now staying with his niece and her husband, Lajoie was to be dead within three years and the seventy year-old Cobb a few more after that. Lajoie said that the two "batted it back and forth for half the day." Among other topics the two spoke about that afternoon were Addie Joss' perfect game, Ty's running, Lajoie's recollections of Lajoie Day in Cleveland in 1912, and his eleven home runs in the 1911 season and about Lajoie's power and his fourteen home runs in 1901.

Wouldn't it have been glorious if during his 75,000 mile odyssey to collect the stories, of the pioneers of baseball, Lawrence Ritter had brought his two reel tape recorder to 188 Daytona Avenue that afternoon? Ironically, the genesis of Lawrence Ritter's game saving idea came with the death of Cobb in 1961. Sadly then, neither Cobb nor Lajoie are included among the old time greats in Ritter's glorious *The Glory of Their Times*. The laughs, the meaningful silences, the savoring and regretful voices of that afternoon will never be heard. What follows is a recreation of what the two might have said, not only on the topics mentioned by Lajoie, but many more. It is liberally sprinkled with actual comments made by each, as extracted from various articles and interviews. It also includes comments previously mentioned.

Previously referred to, the composition book mentioned in the following recreation is one of four such books that contain newspaper clippings that Lajoie carefully cut and pasted to chronicle his career. Interestingly, Lajoie added no commentary to the article content. No words were underlined to stress their importance. No question marks exist to question the veracity of the stories as reported. Without such editorial invasions, it would be up to others to read between the lines, insert their inferences. Lajoie, as said, was not comfortable with making too much of anything.

Just as was Larry's wife, Myrtle, Lillian was a gracious hostess to the visiting parade of writers, past players, family, and fans.

Napoleon Lajoie's former home in Holly Hill, Florida.

"A Day in July"

by Gregory Rubano

Putting aside the small speckled composition book he had been reviewing, Napoleon took a final puff of his pipe. He reminded himself that he would have to tread carefully. One topic was off the table. Ty didn't have to relive any of the gruesome tragedy of his father's death. There are some things that time doesn't heal.

Napoleon Lajoie got up from the rocker and walked through the sweet scent of cherry that filled the air.

"No need to get up, Nap." Dressed in a white shirt and tie, as was Nap, Ty Cobb stood in the entrance of the screened porch attached to the modest white frame ranch.

Nap held out his hand. "Nice of you to come, Ty." The two quickly shook hands as they were to do five or six hours later. The handshakes on parting were longer and accompanied by a pat on the back.

Ty wasn't about to let silence make things awkward. "Place looks nice. You still mowing the lawn? If so, let your nephew do it."

"On occasion, I help Del out. Least I can do." Lajoie laughed. "Ty, we're not all millionaires like you. I suppose if you want, I can find a bell to beckon Lillian."

"Nap, you had the chance to get in on the ground floor with Coke. Hell, I invited you and a few other guys to dinner with my friend from Coke. It was all there for the taking."

Nodding, Nap responded, "Why do you think there's only Pepsi in the fridge?"

"Funny, there you were in that Coke ad telling everyone how much you loved Coke. Why in the world didn't you just push a few hundred dollars across the table and buy their stock? You'd have been a rich man today. Hell, Nap, I've got almost two million in Coke stock. It started at five bucks a share."

Nap stared up at the Spanish moss hanging from the side of the porch. "You know, 100 bucks was a lot of money to me. My mom used to set aside the yolk of an egg once a month to shampoo her hair. Hell, I was lucky to get a mule and a cartoon of chewing tobacco as a signing bonus."

"And now these damned bonus babies get thousands."

"I don't begrudge them their money. Anyway, I'm doing okay. Early on, I made certain I got the stuff. Then, after I got it, I took care of it. One year, my salary went to Somers and his coal business. He paid me 6% interest." Lajoie laughed. "My farm in Mentor had quite a few chickens. Dear old mom could have shampooed her hair ten times a day."

"You are tight as a tick," Cobb responded.

"It's all about using what you were given. I remember one time I flashed my Hall of Fame Gold Lifetime Pass, and the dealer gave me a great discount on a car I was buying for Lilian's husband, Dell."

"You are too much," Cobb replied, shaking his head.

"Look who's talking. A millionaire without electricity and no phone?" Lajoie quickly became conciliatory. "Hey, we both worked hard to earn our money. Played a long time. No need to be spendthrifts. Tell you one thing, though. I made sure no one tried to change the rules in the middle of the game to take advantage of me. Colonel Rogers, for example."

Nap interrupted himself and pointed to the lemonade pitcher. "It's on me. Remember the time I had you over to see if you wanted to invest in Minute Maid?"

Cobb looked puzzled.

"Only kidding, Ty."

Cobb smiled. "You do know Coke's thinking of purchasing Minute Maid?"

"I can't win for losing." Nap saluted Ty with raised glass. "Drink up. Ten bucks a glass."

Ty got up, trying to make it look as effortless as possible. At the serving table, he picked up the pitcher and poured a glass for each of them. "On me. I'll pay you on the way out." He sat down on the floral sofa, eager to renew the discussion. "Colonel Rogers?"

"Yeah. The man loved to make you crawl, a frustrated priest with a confessional in his office. I was ready to return to the Phillies, but he had to start in with how he was going to dock me for non-compliance or some such term he paraded about. 'You will, will you? I'll sell scorecards first,' I yelled at him and stormed out the room."

Lajoie picked up his pipe. "You learn to judge a man by how he treats you when he thinks he's got you down. People like Rogers and Landis thought baseball was gigantic chessboard, and they could move the living pieces as they wished. I can't stomach people that..."

"Landis, that scoundrel." Not surprisingly, Cobb wanted to return to still festering grievances. "All that betting garbage in 1911. He was going to treat me like one of his minions. Man was a tyrant who..."

Lajoie lowered himself effortlessly into his rocker and lit his pipe while Ty raged on like a berserk tea kettle spouting steam. Ten minutes later, Nap brought Ty's tirade to a halt. He had planned this diversion for exactly such an occasion. He rolled up his pant leg to the knee. "Like these calling cards? He pointed to a few spike marks worn now like a badge of honor. "That's you and that's you."

"All that crap about how dirty I played. You think I don't have some of my own? More than you." His legs were scarred with cross hatchings that more than matched Lajoie's in number and depth. "Wonder why I walk like a gimpy dockworker?"

"Hell, Ty, you clawed at my eyes. You screeched like a mad woman."

"All in your imagination. I never played dirty."

"I never said you did," said Nap. "You played hard, possessed."

"It always hurt me to hear that dirty player stuff. A weak spot in whatever armor I have."

"Then why did you wait until you retired to shoot down that story that you stood on the dugout steps sharpening your spikes? I never saw you do that."

"If it meant one moment's hesitation on their part, one second of indecision, I could capitalize upon. You give yourself any chance you can get to claim the prize."

"You brought some of it on yourself then."

"Worth the price. I considered each base a prize to be battled for."

"Think I didn't? You do know I used to move second base farther away from first."

"You conniving Frenchman."

Lajoie finished his lemonade. "Well, I just hope Lillian doesn't come in now. Two old men showing their gams to the world."

It was good to hear Ty laugh, but his lightness didn't last long. "You know, when I came into the league I was a Sunday School choirboy. They turned me into the wildcat snarling to survive. My first year the bastards sawed my bats in half and nailed my spikes to the floor."

When Nap chuckled, Ty glared at him. In a matter of fact voice, Nap said, "Rookies and veterans don't mix, Ty." It was a great cover on Nap's part, for in reality, he was laughing to himself as he conjured images of Ty as a cherubic choirboy. He'd have tripped the others to be the first to the altar.

Ty interrupted Nap's reverie. "Look. I had to fight my whole life to survive. The world was stacked up against me. They tried every lousy trick in the book to whip me, but I beat the bastards and left them in the ditch."

Cobb was certainly the snarling wildcat now.

"Well," Lajoie countered with a steadying voice. "as you once said, it's a game for red blooded men, right? And you ended up on top"

Feeling like a therapist, Larry took a puff of his pipe.

Mollified, Cobb followed, "You know, it's not baseball anymore.

Like the base, Ty believed the plate belonged to the runner.

It's not the game we played. It used to be a science, a game of strategy and applied observation. Now it's the wild swing. Going for the fences with two strikes. No one's head's is in the game, bunch of prima donnas."

"Don't put that Mr. Musial in that category. Saw him play at Daytona Stadium, in '48. I think. He's a great fellow, quiet, attends to his work, minds his own business and stays out of the limelight. A credit to the game."

"Sounds like you."

Lajoie was quick to deflect the compliment, however much he appreciated it. "Ty, you are making too much of all this science thing. For one thing, I never outguessed the pitcher. I was no mind reader. You wanna know what hitting is all about? You go up and hit the ball."

"Stop playing the country bumpkin. Imagine how good you could have been if you applied yourself? I mean, if you had studied hitting, unlocked its secrets."

Lajoie gave Ty a sweeping dismissal with his hand. "I was not in the game to give a spiritualist séance. I do know I never wanted to join the 'chop, chop brigade?' I loved the true sound of a line drive, not the sound of woodpeckers."

It was time to throw a shot at Captain Cobb's bow. "The Flying Dutchman told me once that it wasn't that he had any great faith in his judgement, it just came naturally to figure on those things. Maybe we natural hitters just processed things faster than you."

Nap looked at Cobb's reddening face. They should have called him the Georgia Gamecock, not the Georgia Peach. Even the sagging flesh beneath his chin was red, reminding him of the waddles of his favorite rooster back on the farm in Mentor. It was time to quickly sedate the enraged gamecock. "You are right about the game not being what it was. Our 2-1 games had more bristling action, more stolen bases, more squeeze plays, assists from the outfield, spikings, fist fights and all around hell-raising than these fly ball 14-2 routs have in a week."

Aware that he was preaching to the choir, Nap continued. "And running?" Nowadays, they run like posing roosters. Why steal a base? I'll just stand here till someone knocks me in, if not today, tomorrow. Ho-hum. That reminds me. Ty, did you ever work in the circus?"

"Nap, you've been sipping that lemonade for too long. What are you talking about?"

"I was thinking about how you stole bases. At the last minute, you twisted your whole body and found the unprotected part of the bag. Like an eel. You sure you weren't a contortionist in the off season "

"Well, if I was, you'd be in the tent next to me, flexing. 'Ladies and gentleman, for your viewing pleasure, 'Slashaway, the Strong Man' "

Nap smiled. "I haven't been called *Slashaway* in a while. Hell, Ty, I remember the havoc you caused, forcing guys to throw on to the base ahead to prevent you from stealing the chickens from the henhouse. Of course…"

"Of course, what?" Cobb leaned forward.

"Of course, I knew you were moving second base closer to third." Waiting until Ty smiled a self-congratulatory smile to deliver the clincher, Nap added, "and, of course, under the pretense of holding you on, I'd move it back." Lajoie waited a second. "And more."

It was clear that even now, over forty year later, Ty was trying to reconcile that he had been outsmarted. Mastering such feelings, he replied, "Damn. And I thought you were just a big dumb Frenchman."

"What is good for the goose is good for the gander. All of us played smarter than they do today. We used our brains. We choked up on our bats, considered alternatives, sought to out think the other guy. I shudder to see guys like Greenberg, Foxx, Hack Wilson, Medwick -- all swinging from the heels and going after pitches a foot wide."

Ty stood up and for a moment second baseman Lajoie again felt the presence he often had felt fifty years ago, that foreboding that something was bearing down on you, and you better be ready to defend yourself against the force that claimed what you protected. "Wait just one minute, you French Devil," Ty clamored. "How do you explain some of your crazy swings at balls that were hardly reachable? Some of the stuff you swung the wagon tongue at? Ridiculous. Hell, some were headed towards your head, and you swung!"

Nap prepared to offer his defense, but unpredictably, Cobb offered it for him. "Maybe you just had a better eye than I did." Ty laughed. "I remember that story Ford told about trying to walk you."

"Yeah, I turned his throwaway pitches into doubles, and he finally threw a pitch behind my back and yelled, 'Hit that, you Big Frog.' Later, he told reporters that, fortunately, Lajoie's backside couldn't swing."

"If you weren't hitting that damn dead ball, you would have been the greatest hitter in history. And that's what I told that sportswriter on the *New York Times,* that Daley fellow.' Ty sat up in his chair, as confident in his remark as a preacher pulling back from the podium. "Told him that with the present jack rabbit baseball, Napoleon Lajoie would have set records beyond belief."

Lajoie's silence spoke to his appreciation that the man he considered the greatest player in the history of the game had singled him out and done so in public. "Well, I did hit 14 home runs in 1901." Both men laughed. "But I was no Ty Cobb. You stood above us all."

His own ego assuaged, Cobb asked, "So how many do you think you'd have hit today?"

"One hundred and eleven," said Lajoie, matter-of-factly. "That's what I jokingly told the guy in that American League video I did few years back. It's water over the dam now." Lajoie knew that If ever there was a someone who struggled to accept such a life lesson, it was Cobb.

"I'll tell you, though, it was damn important to me then. The time I went at it with Connolly, demanding that he replace that mushed tomato he called a ball? You know why? I was coming to bat in a few swings and wanted a new ball so I'd have a shot at breaking that home run. Instead, I got thrown out of the game. Of course, so was the ball. I chucked it out of the stadium."

"How many home runs did you hit?" asked Ty.

"Eighty-two."

"I hit one hundred and seventeen." Ty waved his hand in the air. "Home run totals mean nothing. Someday, someone's going to break the Babe's record. Even now, there are guys sitting on the bench who've hit more than fourteen. Injustice to the game."

Nodding, Nap leaned back in the rocker, "You know, Connolly wasn't such a bad guy. Neither was Evans."

"Suppose not, but Evans and I had our moments. Once I challenged him to meet me under the stands after the game."

"To share a few lemonades?" Nap chuckled.

"To his credit, he showed up."

"According to him when he put up his fists, you grabbed him by the tie, pulled him close, and head butted him. He says he was out for a half an hour."

"Well, I got home earlier than expected."

"Did you ever apologize?"

"For what?"

Lajoie said nothing.

"Remember "old wall-eyed, "Catfish" Klem?" asked Cobb.

Lajoie conjured Klem's squinting face from his catalogue of gleaming images. "I know he didn't like that nickname."

"Sure didn't. I remember Evers telling me that once when Catfish was umping, he and Zimmerman had some fun. Evers asked Zim if he had gone fishing on his day off. Zim said, 'Sure did.' Evers asked 'What ya catch?' He was thrown out by Klem before he could say another word."

Lillian entered the room. "Why were you guys showing off your legs? Shame on you. Uncle Larry."

Dell had come in. He was thinking how he'd tell everyone at breakfast that he met Ty Cobb. *"Hey guys, guess what. Ty Cobb came by yesterday to see me."* Dell had a good sense of humor and seemingly a

Catfish Klem

great appetite. He took four chocolate chip cookies from the plate Lilian had brought into the room. He handed a few to Ty. "Mr. Cobb, time for a guided tour of the hacienda. "As Del walked Ty around the small house, he asked Ty his opinion of Ted Williams. Once again, Nap heard the "if only" lecture. When it stopped, Nap knew Ty had slipped away to the bathroom. Nap smiled. He decided against telling Ty that in addition to having a better eye, he had a better bladder.

A few minutes later Ty re-entered the room, standing even as Lillian brought more snacks into the room. Only when Lillian left did he sit down.

Relieved that Ty was staying, Lajoie turned to the page he had bookmarked with a flattened tobacco pouch and handed his composition book to Ty.

"What's this? "

"Just a little book of memories. Look at this one." Nap waited for Ty to scan the article. It was the published letter Cobb had sent to a friend in the middle of the battle for the 1910 batting championship between Ty and Lajoie.

"What are you up? I won that fair and square. Those last few days there was no way I could play."

Nap had purposely put a paper clip connecting the following page. All hell would have broken out if he had seen the article by a Cleveland writer who branded Ty a fraud and coward for sitting out the final games of the season. Nap made sure that a puff of smoke disguised his moving lips as he recited to himself the exact words of the writer. "Ty was suffering from congealed condition of *pedal extremitis* -- cold feet." Nap wondered who would hit the floor first if Cobb read that. That would be embarrassing for Lillian to see as well.

Tyrus Cobb Pays an Eloquent Tribute to Napoleon Lajoie

Winding up a letter to a Cleveland friend, Ty Cobb the great fielder of the Detroit team, says:

My eyes are not very good now and have to use one eye to write

I feel greatly disappointed to go all season so well and then something bob up the last month and throw me out of running for cuts as I realize my eyes may not be right when I go in again and if I am forced out by bad eyes Lajoie will surely beat my present average However I am taking treatment from eye

specialist and tomorrow am going to consult a stomach specialist as it may be caused by stomach trouble as the blur is in front of my right eye causes it not to focus and can only see good from left eye the other is smoky

T. R.

However if I am not to win no better, cleaner contestant could win than Lajoie; he is the one I wish to win it if I cant

Very Truly
Ty. Cobb

Ty Cobb Pays an Elegant Tribute to Napoleon Lajoie

Winding up a letter to a Cleveland friend, Ty Cobb, the great outfielder of the Detroit team, says:

My eyes are not very good now and have to use one eye to write. I feel greatly disappointed to go all season so well and then something comes up the last month and throw me out of the running for the auto as I realize my eyes may not be right when I go in again and if I am forced out by bad eyes Lajoie will surely beat my present average. However, I am taking treatment from eye specialist and tomorrow am going to consult a stomach specialist as it may be caused by stomach trouble as the blur then in front of my right eye causes it not to focus and can only see good from left eye, the other is smoky

T.R.C.

However, if I am not to win no better cleaner contestant could win than Lajoie, he is the one I wish to win it if I can't.

> Very Truly,
> Ty Cobb

"Ty, I won that fair and square too."

Silence. Ty didn't get it. He never would. Watching another ring-let of smoke pass by his head, Cobb said, "Hell, you got a car too."

"I deserved it," Nap said firmly, his own sense of justice violated.

"I got another one the following year," Cobb said, asserting his exclusive claim to the car and to a club Nap would never below to.

Nap threw up his hands in exasperation. "You always thought you were the cat's meow? Hell, Ty, let the other guy have his moment."

Nap rocked himself forward from the rocker and stood up. "I al-ways understood that the one I got ran a lot better than the one they gave you, anyway." It was a good time for Nap to go to the bathroom.

Ty was still in his chair when Nap came back. He was taking a sip of that not- so- good lemonade. Lillian was a sweetheart, but Myrtle made the best lemonade. Thankfully, Cobb had taken no offense to the bitter-ness in Nap's remark nor in the lemonade.

"You know, Nap, I never bought that bunting conspiracy thing. You took what was offered. Played smart. Hell, you were what, 35, 36? You were an old wounded lion, and you fought like one. Gotta respect that."

Ty gazed out the porch, watching nothing. "I am old and tired. All those years of trying to stay ahead of Joe Jackson, Eddie Collins, Babe, and you." He looked appreciatively at Nap.

"I'll say one thing, Ty. It was a helluva battle. I went 23 for 59 until September 18 and added another 21 hits until I got injured. You went 13 for 27 during those last two weeks. In your last 14 games, you went 25 of 48. Of course, you didn't play the last two games."

Impressed by Nap's recital of stats, Ty looked afresh at Nap. He was reliving a season played almost fifty years ago. He realized that Nap wanted to win that batting title more than anything else in the world. If you had to lose, that was the kind of man you should lose to.

Although their batting styles were so different, both Ty and Nap choked up on the bat.

With some guilt, especially after Cobb's flattering remarks, Nap moved away. "Ty, I put that article in my scrapbook because I appreciated what you said about me."

"Maybe I wasn't the bastard everyone thought."

"I know that. Addie's wife told us about that $200 dollars you gave her for the family. And we knew that you were the one that got your teammates on board for the benefit game. I also heard about that fund you are establishing for the kids in Georgia."

Nap thought it was a good time to reach out for the book. He knew he was a turned page away from an apocalypse. Looking down upon the book in his hand, Ty hesitated, and for a moment Lajoie's heartbeat quickened. "It's important to keep these memories, Nap," Ty said, returning the book.

"True. But as much as I kept these press clippings, I didn't allow myself to believe all the flattering drivel."

Ty smiled and patted the rear pocket of his trousers. "I take with me a letter from my father."

Sensing that Ty needed to say more, Nap made a decision to remain silent.

An image of a man before a firing squad crossed Nap's mind. The man was taking a cigarette out of his own pocket.

"He was a great man.' Ty continued. "Did so much with his life and would have done more. I respected him. Hell, he was the only one who mastered me, the only one I ever stepped in line with when he barked orders. Of course, he never got to see me make it big."

"My father, either. My mom did, thank God. I remember the look on her face when I gave first started giving her a $100 a month. Of course, she always put the money aside for that rainy day, but I knew then how proud she was of me."

Suddenly, Nap realized that he had opened the flood gates he had promised himself he would keep shut. *Stupid, stupid, stupid.* Nap didn't know if he should acknowledge his insensitivity, but he did. "I'm sorry, Ty."

Nap bit down on his pipe, unclamped, and tried diversion. "My dad told me baseball players were useless tramps. I suppose a lot of us had to be ready to be disowned. What about your dad?"

Resting on his knee, Ty's finger moved slowly in circles. The wind blew gently into the house on Daytona Avenue:

In front of Walter Cobb was his seventeen year-old son asking to leave home and wanting money to do so. The Augusta club had invited Ty for a try-out, at his own expense, of course. Mr. Cobb was uncharacteristically rational that night. He patiently explained the reality as he saw it. "Ty, the baseball world is full of men who lead a pointless life. Life is all about using your mind." The father explained to the son that education was the key to unlocking mysteries and career possibilities. "I was in military school as a youth. I have connections to West Point."

Each argument dissolved under Ty's protest. "I just have to go."

It was 3 AM. "Well, son, you've chosen. So be it. Go get it out of your system. Let us hear from you once in a while."

Ty looked up at Nap. "When I wrote my father telling him I hadn't made the Augusta club, he wrote back telling me not to come back a failure. There was to be no warm embrace for the prodigal son, and there shouldn't have been."

Nap knew it was time to just listen.

"I've been damn headstrong my whole life. Hell, look at my marriages," said Ty. "But as I said, when my dad gave orders, I stepped in line. Somehow he knew me well. Earlier, he put me in charge of a parcel of the farm, and I loved it."

"You? You loved the farm? Nap laughed heartily. The comic relief was needed. "I was imagining you with a pitch fork in your hand."

"Hold it a moment. No way would I have ever joined you and your chicken raising, shit-tossing local yokels. When a girl I was sweet on came to the farm, I hide in the fields embarrassed that she was going to see me dressed in the dirty farmer overalls." He switched topics in midstream. "Did you know there are ten ways to move, grind, and grade the crop?

"To me, hay is hay. Just give it your best shot. Of course, there is a sweet swing in everything in life, and I was a natural"

Ty caught the humor. "Always, Mr. Science, heh? "

Nap wondered what was in that letter Ty carried.

Done with the back and forth, Ty continued. "My dad knew that I needed to go it alone. No farmhand was going to mentor me. Soon enough, I taught myself the production options, the math of profit and loss, how to deploy resources, even how to pile hay. The best way to do something and everything. And when one day, he took me aside and complimented me on a job well done and asked me if we should sell now or hold on for a better price."

The man facing the firing squad wall took his last puff. "It was the sweetest thing."

Napoleon understood such moments. He took a deep drag on his pipe.

"Soon afterward," continued Ty, "I found myself a job in a cotton factory near town. There I learned the most valuable lesson I ever learned. I learned the value of a dollar and the joy of earning it."

Nap responded quickly. "Silver Spoon, I learned that lesson much earlier than you, while driving a hack through the streets of Woonsocket. I remember when...."

Whether fearing a story that might bring back darker memories or just reminding Lajoie once again that the Georgia Peach was the rooster who announced the morning, Ty cut him off. "Did I ever tell you I am a self-made millionaire?"

An exasperated Lajoie picked up another composition book and turned to a page he had bookmarked with another flattened tobacco pouch. He wanted Ty to see the accolades earned by a son of a cheesemaker -- Addie Joss. Ty took a few seconds to scan the page." Addie was a great guy. And a hell of a pitcher. His perfect game, best game you ever saw?"

"He pitched like a machine that day. I mean I doubt he threw 80 pitches total. Remember how he pitched? Ball coming off that right hip, on top of you all of a sudden. And it wasn't a meaningless game; we were in the middle of a four-way pennant race, you guys included. The fact was Big Ed was on top of his game too. He struck out 15, and the run was un-earned. Passed ball, I think."

"Walsh was damned good."

"Tell me about it. The day after the perfect game I faced him again. I had already hit two doubles, but I also failed to hold on to Harry Bemis' throw and let two runs score in the process. It was all going to be okay though for I came up with the bases loaded and a chance to win it for us.

Big Ed comes in from the bull pen, and on a 3-2 count strikes me out. We lose 3-2, and we end up losing the pennant by a half a game. Know what he struck me out on? Not his bread and butter saliva float. No, he threw me a fast ball down the middle."

"*The Great Lajoie* missed a fastball down the middle?"

"Worse. I took it. Casey of Mudville was a hero compared to me. Casey took a swing and missed. I took a called third strike with the bases loaded."

Before Ty could respond, Lajoie continued. "It's hard to forget those failures. Walsh said years later that it was the highlight of his career. And this is a Hall of Fame guy who won forty games one year."

The jingle of ice cubes. "I would have given a half dozen of the years of my life to win that pennant. Things come around, though. Addie had his number. He also threw a no-hitter against. Big Ed had the audacity to give up one hit that day and lost 1-0. Some call that the greatest pitcher's duel ever. Damn, everything was working that day too. Pity he had to lose."

"There's only one winner, Nap," insisted Ty. "He wasn't as good; no consolation prizes. Anyway, don't feel sorry for Addie. No one can beat perfect. It can't be taken away. You can be 5 for 5, but make an out -- be 5 for 6 -- means failure."

"It's all about risking failure, isn't it Ty?" Replied Nap.
Lajoie's mind sparked. Ty had taken the last few games off in 1910. Hell, some said he went to a Broadway play one night. How bad were those eyes been? Had he been afraid of failure, of coming in second?

Nap couldn't let it go. "One thing about Ted Williams," he told himself, "he wasn't going to back into any award. Impressive stuff to refuse to sit out the final game of the doubleheader when his .400 average was on the line."

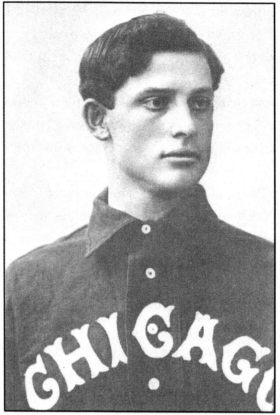

Big Ed Walsh

Finally, Lajoie looked up, knowing he was taking too big a lead to be entertaining such thoughts about Cobb. "Ty, a perfect game for a pitcher is out of his hands, an error by a teammate, failure to cover the bag quick enough, whatever. Addie threw four one hitters. He could have applied all the science in the world to his pitching, and the difference would still have been some punk hit, a Baltimore Chop or maybe a fielder with slightly slow reflexes. Hell, I cost Bush a no-hitter that last year with the A's. I should have had that grounder, a younger second baseman would have."

"At least Addie's deeds are inscribed on his Hall of Fame plaque," Cobb replied.

"And three years later, after his perfect game, Addie's dead, and his two kids and wife get the box score of the game."

Nap often thought of his friend. *One of a kind, a gentle soul. It would have been so wonderful to stand on that Hall of Fame podium with him. To go in together is how it should have ended.*

Nap rubbed his chin. "Did you know Addie had forty shutouts in his career? So would you rather have 41 shutouts or be beloved by players and fans alike, as was Addie?

Placing his index and fore finger onto his lip, Cobb put his thumb under his chin. "Let me think it over," responded Cobb. Seeing Lajoie's quizzical look, he laughed. "You don't "remember the Jack Benny sketch when the robber asks him, 'Your money or your life?' And Jack puts his finger and thumb under his chin and says, 'Let me think it over a minute.'

It was good to see that Ty had some self-effacement in him. "Okay, your minute is up, Mr. Benny."

"How about you make it 45 shutouts?" laughed Ty. "I'll tell you one thing. They don't have his kind of pitcher around today."

"Don't tell that to Mr. Williams. He contends that modern hitters face better pitchers than we did. I made the case in the paper for Walsh, Mathewson, Young, and Johnson. I do think this Mr. Feller's a close second to our Walter."

"All this from a guy who refuses to adjust his hitting when they put that shift on him."

"Ty, you'd hit .800 against that shift. Hell, you even hit well against the Big Train."

"That's because I knew he was afraid of hitting a batter with that thunderous fastball. So I moved closer to the plate and could reach his strikes on the corner."

"Old Walter was something else. I remember when Chapman had a second strike called against Johnson and started to walk away.

Having fun with Cy Young who said of Nap, "He was the Babe Ruth of our time."

When the ump told him he still had one coming, he told him to take it, he didn't want it.

"To walk away from a battle? What kind of player is that?"

Lajoie ignored the comment. Ty couldn't have forgotten that Chapman was killed by a pitched ball. "Walter once hit a guy's cap with his fastball, and it turned right around on his head."

Ty wasn't about to be diverted. "If only Walter had that last ounce of combativeness."

"And if only he wasn't such a nice guy," interrupted Lajoie. "Hell,

Ty, Walter was great. Period."

Larry looked down on all the ring marks from all the glasses of lemonade. Lillian wanted to replace the table or at least refinish it, but Nap insisted the rings remain. That one came from Fred Merkle's glass, and those from Al and his charming wife from Woonsocket. Wish that one could have been Addie's. So many. Even as he spoke to familiar faces swirling ghostlike in the smoke, Nap's eyes returned to Cobb. "Just once, I would have loved to taste the champagne. I would have given anything to raise that toast to my teammates just once. I guess it wasn't meant to be. Like when I got blood poisoning from being spiked. Until I got hurt, we were in the hunt."

"What was it, the dye from the black stocking? I remember the photo of you in a wheelchair."

"The doctors told me they might have to amputate the leg if the infection didn't leave. Everyone since wears white sanitary understockings. Maybe I saved someone's life." Lajoie smiled half-heartedly. "A consolation prize, as you would say."

Mr. Empathy, Cobb was not. "We won three pennants, but...."

"Don't say "but" to a man who never won one."

"But," Ty persisted, "I never won a World Series championship. O for 3."

"You were still wet behind the ears. You couldn't have been but twenty-three in the last one."

Ty corrected him. "Twenty two. I kept on trying till the very end."

Lajoie laughed. "So we both spent our final years with the A's trying to see if we could a sip of Mr. Mack's championship wine. Pretty pathetic."

"And when I left, they won it. Two years in a row." Exasperated, Ty fired away, "If you and Somers hadn't turned down the trade, we'd both be showing our World Series rings."

Lajoie knew what he meant by "the trade." "Just stupid. I think about that more than I do the Coke deal. Can you imagine what I felt when you dressed in a Nap uniform at the Addie Benefit? Tell me the truth, were you stickin' it to me?"

"I didn't pack my uniform. I had a cold and didn't think I'd be playing.

"And travel connections to Cooperstown made you miss the Induction ceremony?"

"I wasn't about to have my picture taken with Landis. None of them played the game, they just..."

Nap derailed Ty. "Remember, Nigel Clarke?" Lajoie shook his head. "Just a stubborn old Frenchman."

Baseball's first commissioner, the tyrannical Kenesaw Landis,
suspended Cobb for alleged betting.

Confused, Cobb asked, "Clarke was French?"

"No. One day Nigel came to me asking to have a day off to visit his wife who he had just married. I refused, and we had words. The next day during warmups, he turned the back of his catching hand to a fastball, held the bleeding hand up and announced, 'Guess I have the day off to see my wife.' He was out for months. Not the best move by Manager Lajoie."

"Don't talk good of Clarke. He told me that a good number of times he missed the tag on me and others, but his god-damn quick hands conned the ump. Cost me a dozen or so putouts!"

"Ty, you already have the record by a lot."

Cobb said nothing. "Well, we came to fists over it."

Lajoie looked at the tormented man sitting in the late afternoon light. "Ty, I wouldn't want to be you."

Ty responded, "Nap, if only you had had that last ounce of combativeness."

Both men laughed. As soon as the laughter passed, Ty moved his chair closer. "Tell me about that day in Cleveland in 1912."

"The biggest kick out of all my baseball days. They brought out a gigantic horseshoe of gleaming silver dollars. The fans had donated 1,009 of them. I don't have to tell you that was dough. Look at the prices. What was a pound of coffee? Fifteen cents?"

The two talked of the price of sugar and about cars and the novelty of telephones. In the midst of their discussion about bathrooms back then, Nap suddenly broke into song. "Ah! sweet mystery of life…." He stopped and pointed at Cobb, who immediately figured out the game. "At last I've found you." Cobb began the next contest: "Let me call you sweetheart." Quicker than he sent the fielded ball on its way, Lajoie responded, "You belong to me." After a few rounds, now in the lead by one, Cobb decided to pay his respects to Lillian. Lajoie knew why the competition had stopped when it did. He almost blurted out, "What, your eyes need a rest?"

As he heard Ty exchanging pleasantries with Lillian, another very popular song popped into his head, "I Want a Girl Just Like the Girl Who Married Dear Old Dad." Once again, Nap thought how hard it must be to be Ty Cobb.

It was time to go to the bathroom. As soon as Nap returned, the two again crossed the white lines.

"Seen any of the guys?"

"Fred Merkle and I talk enough, watching the Little League kids

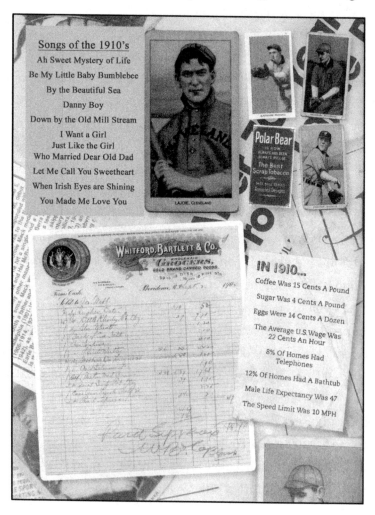

play. Good guy. He got a raw deal. McGraw considered him one of the brightest players he had. He made a mistake. Would you want a nickname *Bonehead* to follow you to the grave? The game can be cruel. Anyway, Merk tells a great story about McGraw. Passed on by Rube Marquard. Seems the Little Round One was giving Ump Hurst quite the time, calling him a blind so and so, and more. When Muggsy screamed that the pitch Hurst had just called a ball was where the previous strike was called, Hurst responded, "If you say so, Muggsy." He then called Muggsy out on strikes."

"Muggsy was something else. You and he together would have been match and dynamite. Rube told about a Giant teammate who after hitting a home run to win the game was confronted by the General demanding to know why he hadn't sacrificed as ordered. The player, think it was Murray, explained that he cowtailed it over the fence since the pitch was "right in the gut." McGraw asked him again where the pitch was, fined him 100 bucks and told him, "You can put that right in your gut too."

Nap the storyteller was on a roll. "Seems Rube's father was something else. He had no use for baseball. Told Rube there was no money in it. That he didn't understand why a grown man would want to wear funny looking suits. When Rube followed his dream, he and his split. Father didn't speak to him for 10 years. Then one day, an older guy shows up at the clubhouse to see him. It's his father, of course. The guy had watched Rube pitch, and rejoiced in his son's success. Knew nothing about baseball. Told Rube he sat behind the guy "wearing a funny thing on his face." Didn't know the name for first base either. Later, he gets interviewed and tells reporters that as a kid he used to love to play baseball. Said he was a pitcher, like his son."

Ty felt like a theatergoer as Larry's reels of memories crossed the screen. It was time for him to contribute to the discussion. "All I know is that Rube was a pitcher, a member of a fraternity that tried to take our meal ticket."

Nap responded, "We are all in the same fraternity now. Ty, remember Bugs Raymond-the great spitballer who loved his booze?

Ty nodded.

"Rube said that Raymond didn't have to spit on the ball. He would just breath on it, and the ball would come up drunk."

"Another waste of ability. Another guy who had no discipline. Big Ed's slobbered sphere was better anyway."

"Agreed."

"Did you ever see *Wee Willy* play then?

"Keeler? No."

"I forgot how young you are. He was inducted with us, posthumously, of course. He reminded me a lot of you. Scrappy guy, fighting for every break. Great bat control. Hit to all fields." Lajoie laughed, "And like you, a clever bastard. He could drop a bunt on a handkerchief, and then when we'd move in, he'd slam a line drive over our heads. The cranks loved him."

"Of course, there was the time I embarrassed him, and hit a pitch intended to be a ball, way outside. I drove it to right field. Keeler must have been thinking it was ball four; anyway he was asleep at the wheel. The ball hit him straight in the chest and almost knocked him over. Inning later he hits a double and arriving at the base he had some delicate words for me. I can only imagine if it had been you."

"It wouldn't have happened to me, Anyway, a guy falls asleep on the field deserves what he gets. He must have known you had a batting habit of going for those way-out-of- the pond pitches. 'Study your foes. And they're all your foes.' I always said. Tried to pass that advice on when I managed. Some listened, most didn't."

Nap pulled out a clip from his scrapbook. "Cut this out. It's from one of those baseball in the old days, way back, 1886. Outfielder name Powell was chasing a deep drive when a nearby dog that had been sleeping joined him in the chase. The dog bit Powell and wouldn't let go. The hit went for a game winning inside-the park home run, Reminded me of you. We learned not to rouse the sleeping dog Cobb. You would never let go."

Ty smiled. "My throat's a little dry. Could you get me a Coke? I mean a Pepsi."

"You bush leaguer, I ought to...."

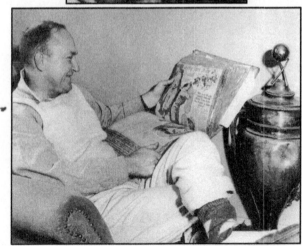

A familiar sight: Nap reviewing his scrapbooks.
Ty had his own scrapbook, but the pride of accomplishment wasn't enough.

Outside, the palm trees started to sway in the warm late afternoon breeze; a storm was coming, always did around this time. There would be time later to deal with the inevitable.

"I felt a faint sorrow. It suddenly dawned on me that here in the theatre of his brain, Napoleon was conjuring up long buried heroes. He was reeling off nicknames, repeating decades of slang, mimicking conversations of bully boys whose spike prints have long been raked over…one day these old baseball heroes will no longer perform because there will be no one to conjure them up. One by one, the little theatres will be darkened."

-- Jimmy Powers, following a 1939 interview with Napoleon Lajoie

In Ty Cobb's Shadow

Now summer goes
And tomorrow's snows
Will soon be deep,
And the sky of blue,
Which summer knew
Sees shadows creep.
As the gleam tonight
Which is silver bright
Spans ghostly forms,
The winds rush by
With a coming cry
Of coming storms.
So the laurel fades
In the snow-swept glades
Of flying years,
And the dreams of youth
Find the bitter truth
Of pain and tears.
Through the cheering mass
Let the victors pass
To find fate's thrust
As tomorrow's fame
Writes another name
On drifting dust.

A poem kept in the wallet of Bill Wambsganss who had cut it out from a New York paper he was reading on the elevated train going up to the Polo Grounds. A shortstop, Wambsganss was replaced by Ray Chapman, the only professional player to be killed by a pitched ball. Wambsganss played with Napoleon Lajoie and the Cleveland Naps.

From *The Glory of Their Times.*

References

Books:

Alexander, Charles. *Ty Cobb*. London: Oxford University Press, 1984.

Alexander, Charles. *Our Game: An American Baseball History*. New York: Henry Holt, 1991.

Bak, Richard. *Ty Cobb: His Tumultuous Life and Times*. Texas: Taylor Publishing Company, 1994.

Barlett, Arthur. *Baseball and Mr. Spalding*. New York: Farrar, Strauss and Young, Inc., 1951.

Cobb, Ty. *My Life in Baseball: The True Record*. Garden City: Doubleday, 1961.

Daley, Arthur. *Times at Bat*. New York: Doubleday, 1971.

Epstein, Sam. *More Stories of Baseball Champions in the Hall of Fame*. Illinois: Garrard Publishing Company, 1973.

Kashatus, William. *Money Pitcher: Chief Bender and the Tragedy of Indian Assimilation*. University Park, Pennsylvania: Pennsylvania State University Press, 2006.

Lieb, Fred. *Baseball as I have Known It*. New York: Gossett and Dunlap, 1977.

Meany, Tom. *Baseball's Greatest Players*. New York: Gossett and Dunlap Publishing, 1953.

Murphy, James. *Napoleon Lajoie: Modern Baseball's First Superstar*. SABR, 19

Okrent, Daniel. *Baseball Anecdotes*. New York: Oxford University Press. 1989.

Powers. Jimmy. *Baseball's Personalities (The Most Colorful Figures of All Time)*. New York: Rudolph Field, 1949.

Radar, Benjamin. Baseball: A History of America's Game Urbana: Unioversity of Illinlis Press, 1992.

Ritter, Lawwrence. *The Glory of Their Times: The Story of the Early Days of Baseball Told by the Men Who Played It. New York:* MacMillan Company, 1966.

Ritter, Lawrence and Donald Honig, *The Image of Their Greatness*. New York: Crown Publishers, , 1979.

Seymour, Harold. *Baseball: the Early Years*. New York: Oxford University Press, 1960.

Stern, William. *Bill Stearn's Favorite Baseball Stories*. Garden City, New York: Blue Ribbon Books, 1949.

Sullivan, Dean. *Early Innings*. Lincoln, Newbraska: University of Nebraska Press, 1995.

Voigt, David Quentin. *American Baseball from the Commissioners to Contintental Expansion*. Pennyslvania: Pennsylvania State University Press. 1983.

Articles

"Billy Evans Says," Bismarck Tribune, February 2, 1923.

Bobrick, M.A. "Lajoie- the Man," Base Ball Magazine, June, 1908.

Broeg, Robert." Lajoie Smooth as Silk, Poison at Bat," Sporting News, August, 1963.

Brook, Hal. "Leaving Ty in a Bind," Elyria Chronicle Telegram, June 3, 1995.

Cobb, Ty. "They Don't Play Baseball Anymore," Life XXXII (March 17, 1952).

"Tricks That Won Me Ball Games," Life XXXII (March 24, 1952).

"Cobb Awarded Batting Title," Washington Post, October 16, 1910.

Crane, Sam. "Lajoie Born Ball-Player Declares Crane," New York Evening Journal, July, 1917.

Croy, Homer." "Cleveland's Famous Second Baseman," Oelwein Daily Register, March 22, 1912.

Daley, Arthur. " Typographical Error," New York Times, May 22, 1955.

Daniel, Dan. "Georgia Peach Unhappy," Newport Daily News, May 2, 1955.

Drohan, John. " 'Cobb Could Have batted .800 Against Williams Shift'-- Lajoie," Daytona News, August, 1955.

"Eberfield Declares Lajoie Hardest Hitter of All," Cedar Rapids Republican, July 6, 1913.

Edwards, Henry. " Supermen of Ring and Diamond: Cobb and Lajoie,"

"Fans Are Royal," Mansfield News, July 25, 1911.

Fraley, Oscar. " Late Nap Lajoie Great Fan of 'Georgia Peach' " Eureka Humboldt Standard, July 18, 1961.

Grahame, Arthur. "Big Frenchy: Napoleon Lajoie's Own Story," Sport Story Magazine, Street and Smith, 1939.

Greene, Greg. " Something to Think About," Woonsocket Call, April 10, 1957.

Grayson, Harry. " Standout Prospect Was Lucky to be Given Bicycle," The Independent Record, March 5, 1950.

"Lajoie Had Gallic Grace," Berkshire Evening Eagle, April 6, 1948.

Holland, David. "The One and Only Cobb," American Mercury LXXXIII (September,1956).

"How Lajoie Started," Elyria Evening Telegram, May 11, 1907.

"I Remember," the Sporting News, November 4, 1953.

"Lajoie-Cobb Race for Title in 1910 Led to Inquiry by League President," Sporting News, August 23, 1950.

"Lajoie Dies at 83; King of Second Baseman," the Sporting News, February 18, 1959.

"Lajoie, King of Baseball, Grants Sunday Post an Interview, "Boston Sunday Post, May 22, 1904.

"Lajoie Makes a Loan,"Washington Post, November

"'Lajoie the Greatest Batter.' says Cobb," Waterloo Times Tribune, November 6, 1910.

Lardner, Ring W. "Tyrus, the Greatest of 'Em All," American Magazine, LXXIX (June 15, 1915)

"Larry as a Umpire Killer," Washington Post, February 3, 1907.

"Larry Lajoie with Old Baseball, Says Present Batting Averages Would Shrink," Ogden Examiner, March 9, 1950.

MacFarlane, Paul. " After 70 Years, Researchers Prove Lajoie Really Did Win," Sporting News, August 18, 1981.

"Memorial for Joss," Oshkosh Daily Northwestern, July 24, 1911.

"Nap Lajoie, Baseball Great Laid to Rest," Daytona Beach Evening News, February 8, 1939.

"Nap Lajoie Located," Christian Post, May 29, 1939.

"Napoleon Lajoie: Emperor of the Realm of Baseball,"Boston Sunday Globe, July 20, 1902.

"Napoleon Lajoie of Fall River," Swan River Star, June 1, 1904.

O'Connell, Fred. "Lajoie," Boston Sunday Post, May 2, 1904.

Pope, Edwin, "Dollar Deluge Lite Lajoie Life," Miami Herald, March 21, 1957.

Powers, Jimmy, "Bill Klem, Umpire Since 1902, Places Five Moderns on All-Time, All Star Baseball Team," Chicago Daily Tribune, February 26, 1939.

Powers, Jimmy. "Powerhouse," New York Daily News, February 18, 1939.

"Proud of Son's Fame," Washington Post, July 29, 1906.

Rice, Grantland. "Lajoie and Grace," Newport Daily News, July, 1916.

"Rivalry of Two Stars of the Diamond: Premier Batters, Cobb and Lajoie," Waterloo Evening Courier, February 11, 1911.

Royal, Chip,"Mack Selects Early Day Stars," Port Arthur News, March 20, 1944.

"The Story of Petie," Boston Sunday Post, August 24, 1902.

"There's No Such thing as a Batting Slump Says the Mighty Lajoie of the Cleveland Naps," The New York Press, September 26, 1910.

" Tribute of William Sunday to the Work and Life of Adrian Joss," Waterloo Evening Courier, April 24, 1911.

"Unknown Wives of Well-Known Men," Des Moines Daily News, April 8, 1909.

Weir, Hugh. "Larry Lajoie-The Man Who Breaks Baseballs" The American Boy, July 1908.

Whitney, Eugene. " Scuffed Ball with Emery to Help Hurlers in Tricks Permanently Framed in Flailing Frenchman's Mental Gallery," Cleveland Plain Dealer, 1915.

"Worthy of Our Affection," Atlanta Constitution, August 23, 1914.

All photos used in this book were provided from the vast personal collection of the author.

Author's Note

I am most indebted to James Murphy's *Napoleon Lajoie: Modern Baseball's First Superstar*. It was a constant reference and inspiration. The first attempt to resurrect public awareness of Lajoie, the book must be part of any Lajoie fan's library. Also to the wonderful stories told by baseball's early stars in Lawrence Ritter's *The Glory of Their Times: The Story of the Early Days of Baseball Told By The Men Who Played It*. And to Arthur Daley's *Times at Bat* for more tales of the diamond. Richard Bak's *Ty Cobb: His Tumultuous Life and Times* shined a revealing and focused light on Cobb, as did Charles Alexander's *Ty Cobb*. A wealth of historical perspective on baseball's culture and times was provided by David Quentin Voigt's *American Baseball: From the Commissioners to Continental Expansion* and Harold Seymour's *Baseball: The Early Years*.

The Hall of Fame's very helpful research staff offered access to a wealth of archival materials, including Lajoie's scrapbooks.

As I collected the many stories and recollections of players and writers of Lajoie's era, I realized that in some cases confirmations would be problematic. For one thing, those who saw an event offer but their own version of the event. Further complications arise when the remembrances of those who participated in that event sometimes change as time goes on. Embellishments and recreations are common as players, fans, and reporters massaged stories to fit agendas. In addition, early nineteenth century reporters rarely had the inclination or resources to check on the stories written by their peers and so they passed on what they have been told or read and hearsay evidence became evidence. As expected then, research often reveals nuances, omissions, and contradictions in recall. Sometimes it is easy to see an error has been made. For example, Lajoie mentions that when Ty Cobb visited him in Florida, among other things, they talked about Lajoie's 11 home runs in 1911. In

1911, Lajoie hit but two home runs. The gist of the discussion was clear, nevertheless. The two discussed the merits or lack of the modern worship of the home run. Somethings, however, will always be clouded. Did Lajoie sign his first professional contract on the back of an envelope as many contended? A case can be made that he might not have. Yet, the integrity of Lajoie and the situation surrounding the signing suggests he may have. Did Lajoie beat the living daylights out of the ball against the pitcher whose later recommendation opened his path to professional ball? The pitcher says he did. Lajoie says he did. The boxscores show Lajoie to be hitless against the pitcher. Were there other games between the two not represented by boxscores? Most likely, we'll never know. Stories about Waddell. as they are for Cobb and Wagner and many others, are legion. Did Waddell gather his fielders together and have them sit while he struck out the side? If so, only in exhibition games? in the ninth inning? And what of the many exploits of showman Satchell Paige years later? I came to appreciate that the stories in themselves are stories. And that lore is a collection of stories dusted with truth, imagination and mythology.

One baseball historian has proclaimed that "...the early history of modern major league baseball is filled with funny, fantastic, and fabulous stories. Some of them are true." Perhaps it is better to add that they are all filled with truths, and that many offer fantastic insights into the personalities of those with whom they are associated. It is also important to remember that such 3-F stories did not stop with the closing of the Dead Ball Era. They continue to be part of the imaginative fabric of the game, passed on from one generation of fans and players to the next. A case in point. In the late 70's, interviewer Dick Cavett gathered on his show Hank Aaron, Leo Durocher, Umpire Tom Gorman, and Mickey Mantle to discuss the game they loved. The importance of a good tale, a shared history, immediately became apparent when Mickey

Mantle launched into the story of Dizzy Dean's betting Hank Greenberg before a 1934 World Series game against the Tigers that Dean would strike him out every time he faced him After striking out his first three at-bats, Greenberg managed to pop a foul ball off the plate. As the catcher settled under it, Dean intentionally shoved him out of the way, and the ball fell to the ground. A few pitches later, Greenberg had again struck out, and Dean had won his bet. Having told the story with gusto, Mickey waited until the laughter died down and sheepishly asked Dean's Gas House Gang teammate, Durocher, "Is that right? I heard it, but I don't believe it." Durocher nodded and mumbled some response, but the answer didn't matter; the story did. Of course, it was Durocher's turn to tell some of his stories. One included the story of Umpire Bill "Catfish" Klem, so named according to Durocher because " he looked like a catfish." As an anecdote in the final chapter of this book reveals, Klem always took great offense at the nickname, and many batters of a few eras returned to the bench when they so provoked him. On this occasion, an unidentified fan had aimed a steady stream of piscine references at Klem. Frustrated that he couldn't locate the offender, Klem asked batter Durocher to do so for him. Glad to oblige, Leo rather dramatically pointed at the miscreant in the stands. Upset that Durocher had stood there and pointed rather than deliver the message with more subtlety, Klem threw Durocher out of the game. Even Durocher admitted that it was the only time he hadn't deserved to be thumbed. Good story, Leo. Your turn, Hank.

About the Author

A long-time educator who earned his doctorate at the University of Connecticut, Greg Rubano has recently published two books for middle school youth about inspirational figures in baseball history. *Freedom Between the Lines* dramatizes Native Americans' use of baseball to confront the crippling prejudice of the federal government's boarding school attempt to "civilize" them. It focuses upon the struggles and startling accomplishments of Charles Albert Bender, the only Native American player in the Hall of Fame. *Before the Babe, the Empero: Napoleon Lajoie,* brings alive a young mill boy's worship of the American League's first superstar- Napoleon Lajoie. The books and presentations are part of a Rhode Island campaign: *Unearthing our Treasure: Napoleon Lajoie.*

In an attempt to resurrect interest and appreciation of the game among all ages, Greg has spoken to middle school, college and museum audiences about America's pastime. He is also an instructor for WriteOnSports, a youth-targeted literacy program to use baseball to inspire reading and writing.